THE LUMONICS THEATER

Other Wildside Press Books

Nourathar: The Art of Light-Color Playing
Mary Hallock-Greenewalt

The Complete Patents
Mary Hallock-Greenewaltt

Colour-Music
A. Wallace Rimington

Structuring Time: notes on making movies
Michael Betancourt

Metaphors on Vision
Stan Brakhage

THE LUMONICS THEATER
THE ART OF MEL & DOROTHY TANNER

EDITED BY MICHAEL BETANCOURT

Wildside Press

Mel & Dorothy Tanner in Haloween Costumes, 1970

Wildside Press
www.wildsidepress.com

CONTENTS

HISTORY & DEVELOPMENT

Mel Tanner's light cubes circa 1967.

THE LUMONICS THEATER

Michael Betancourt

The name "*Lumonics*" describes a theatrical show that combines environmental sculptures with kinetic painting, and ultimately video. The origins of the title for the production begins with the combination of the words "luminous" and "harmonics" in a magazine review of the first shows written by Dave Robbins in 1970.[1] However, over the years Mel and Dorothy Tanner told a variety of different origin stories to the media, ranging from the Latin work "lumen,"[2] meaning "light," to being adopted from Jane Robert's novel *Seth Speaks*.[3] Dorothy has also identified the origin as a transcendental experience of Mel's outside *Hi-Fi Associates* in 1969 reported during the interviews for the creation of this history. The variety of stories reflects an interest in invention and re-invention that makes any history written about *Lumonics* necessarily tentative and potentially unreliable.

Mel Tanner's belief in the importance and centrality of light to human experiences and understanding reiterates the equivalence of light and understanding in the English language. Dorothy tells a story about the "birth" of the theater in 1969 while she and Mel were creating audio-visual installations for home theaters:

> "Mel had an experience in the parking
> lot of Hi-Fi Associates and was changed by
> the light glinting off the wing of an airplane.
> He saw himself on the other side of the
> parking lot and knew the *Lumonics* theater
> was the way to go." [Dorothy]

This is a mythological beginning suitable for any Modern art: the idea for *Lumonics* comes from a moment of transcendent experience caused by the light reflecting off the aluminum wing of an airplane passing overhead in flight. The original name of the theater, *After Image*, — a ghost image burned into the human retina from seeing a sudden, bright light, such as a flash from a camera strobe — implies a degree of truth to Dorothy's story. But the important feature in her story is the role of light as a transformative force for enlightenment. While Dorothy implies a sudden moment of insight, the "bolt out of the blue" coming off the airplane wing, as provoking an instantaneous transformation, the development of their work prior to the beginning of the theater suggests something different: the *Lumonics* theater did not begin as a bolt out of the blue, but instead comes from a series of gradual developments that collectively enable Mel's moment of inspiration.

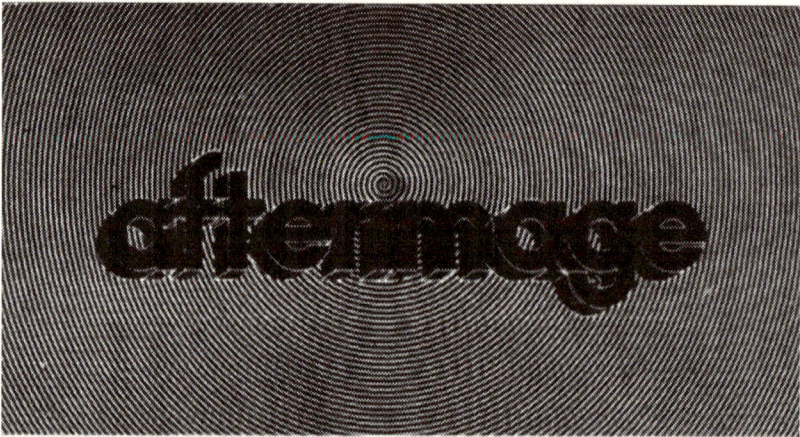

355 NE 59TH TERRACE ☐ PHONE 759-1312

The concerns of the first phase begin a process that moved the theater away from its origins in psychedelic light shows and towards the complex form of the later phases of *Lumonics*. This total art work produced by *Lumonics* comes from a distinct approach, different from the earlier avant-gardes' application of a uniform aesthetic to a variety of media. Instead of taking different media and subjecting them to a single, uniform aesthetic—assemblage, collage, Constructivism, Surrealism, etc.—the Tanners constructed their work in this first phase with the goal of incorporating the individual pieces into a performance, either as a part of the screen (the sculpture called "The Sun" marks the center of it), an object in the environment, or as a lightbox contributing to the performance directly. The concept which unifies these works is their role in the concert.

The Tanners interest in directing and changing the consciousness of their concert audience is not only a feature of the origins in the early 1970s. It is a crucial motivating factor in the development and expansion of the parameters defining the theater, and should be understood as a guiding principle for the development of the theater as a whole, a principle that fosters the gradual movement towards becoming a gesamtkunstwerk. Many of these expansions are the direct result of input from the team of assistants that joined the Tanners when the theater formally organized itself in1972. These assistants, especially Marc Billard, moved *Lumonics* towards being a self-contained art form through their ideas about how to create an emotionally real experience inside the theater.

Lumonics has been active since 1969. In the more than thirty years of its existence, it has transformed itself several times, changing from a live, virtuoso visual improvisation into an environment installed in an art gallery, and back into a theatrical concert that uses both video and unique technologies for creating abstract real-time visuals. In doing so, it has followed the same path as the historical avant-garde in its search for a large, receptive audience, and participated in romanticism's search for the mythical

a new direction in sound

Progress in the field of music reproduction has been evolutionary. This week we believe we will begin showing an intertwining between stereo music equipment, sculpture, lighting and color that well may be revolutionary. Fine music moves toward a total experience by adding form and color to the aural sensation. There are no limitations in the total effect possible — so wide is the scope that an entire room has been prepared for demonstration, using McIntosh and J.B. Lansing sound equipment. This new concept provides a total emotional impact that is difficult to describe adequately. The present announcement can only be an invitation to visit Hi-Fi Associates Biscayne Boulevard showroom on the special opening nite. You will see and hear the definitive combination of music, form and color in total envelopment.

new directions in environment

Color, space, furnishings, light, and even sound are all factors in the total feel of any human habitation. People have worked over the years with a limited range of possibilities. This is equally true with many contemporary homes. Now at Hi-Fi Associates' Light and Sound studio you will see advanced concepts in manipulating total environment. Emotional effects that can be changed in moments, rather than over months with major alterations in decor. Consider a room that might contribute to the evening's entertainment rather than just contain it. It's at hand now.

a new direction in art

It is a matter of common knowledge that there is a crisis in art. It would appear that the crisis is a symptom of the struggle towards new means of expression as well as attempts to master new materials. Mel and Dorothy Tanner, whose work is featured in the new marriage of sound and art, are well known artists and sculptors. Trained at Pratt Institute, Cooper Union, Brooklyn Museum and having exhibited in galleries in Europe and America, the Whitney Museum and N.Y.U., they have worked for months with sound and lighting engineers at Hi-Fi Associates to bring this new art form to fruition. It may well be that the special showing March 20th is an important step in a new direction.

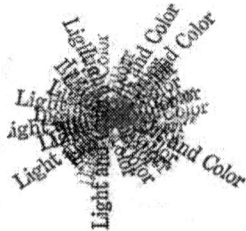

a new dimension in Sound...

Special opening: Thursday evening, March 20, 7:30-10 P.M.

3180 BISCAYNE BLVD. MIAMI

Hi-Fi Associates' promotional flyer for the Tanner's light-sound work in Miami, 1969.

gesamtkunstwerk, or total art work, using all the existing arts to create a singular, transcendent aesthetic experience from purely abstract, visual materials.

The *Lumonics* theater began as a visual performance inspired by experiments done by Mel and Dorothy Tanner with a color organ, and by the psychedelic light shows popular in rock concerts during the 1960s. Its influence on the evolution of *Lumonics* is significant, since instead of pursuing film or video, it led to their work with live imaging, in a direct manipulation of light.

Light is the unifying principle of Mel's conception of *Lumonics* as a transformative practice. What these performances reveal is the significance of time and the movement of light in the audience's experience of the work. It is this added dimension that enables the effacement of the boundaries between different arts through the manipulation of light:

> "Once people understand that they can
> control their environment and their lives
> through light they'll have some idea of the
> awareness that we're trying to project here,
> " says Mel.
> "The whole idea behind everything here
> is to take light and make it into a shape. A
> shape that not only solidifies the light but
> the life the light touches."[4]

In his art it becomes the central material that determines the shape, form and meaning of the individual sculptures. The lighted acrylic sculptures are component parts of a total environment, not as individual art objects in the traditional sense; their function as art objects independent of their role in the theater is similar to the aesthetic role performed by altar pieces that once performed a different role in a church. The aesthetic that guides *Lumonics* is one of sensory envelopment, a result of collections of artworks functioning environmentally. Their meaning comes from their role in the theater itself. Each sculpture, instead is a modular component in the larger construction, the *Lumonics* theater. While they can be encountered independent of the theater, the type of experience these art objects present requires a reconstruction of their relationship to the whole. This theater passed through six distinct phases over the thirty years of its existence. For the first five stages of its development, *Lumonics* was built around live performance by Mel and Dorothy Tanner who would manipulate masks, slides and kaleidoscopes, as well as produce kinetic paintings using acrylic trays placed on overhead projectors, and focused onto the same screen. This meant that no two performances could ever be the same.

It was only in the sixth phase (beginning in 1999 when Marc Billard purchased a video projector) that video began to play a role in the actual concert performances themselves. Prior to this period, video was used before or after the performance, in a space separate from the main theater, as a supplement. Beginning as early as 1980, *Lumonics* offered a videotape for sale as a way to extend beyond its theater.

However, inspite of its incorporation of real objects and actual space into the performances, *Lumonics* has always been constructed as a proscenium with an essentially flat screen. In the center of that screen is a small, circular sculpture called "The Sun" whose flat blades are oriented perpendicular to the screen, acts to prismatically alter the projected light, emerging from the projection at one moment, then vanishing into it at another. The importance of this sculpture to the performances becomes obvious through a comparison to the videos based upon the shows. Each *Lumonics* tape was created and conceived as a separate kind of show than those produced live, and in every case, the video was recorded using a flat screen placed much closer to the projectors than the one used for the show. This difference was partially a technical requirement imposed by the ability of the video cameras to pick-up the image, but the result was a very different kind of image be-

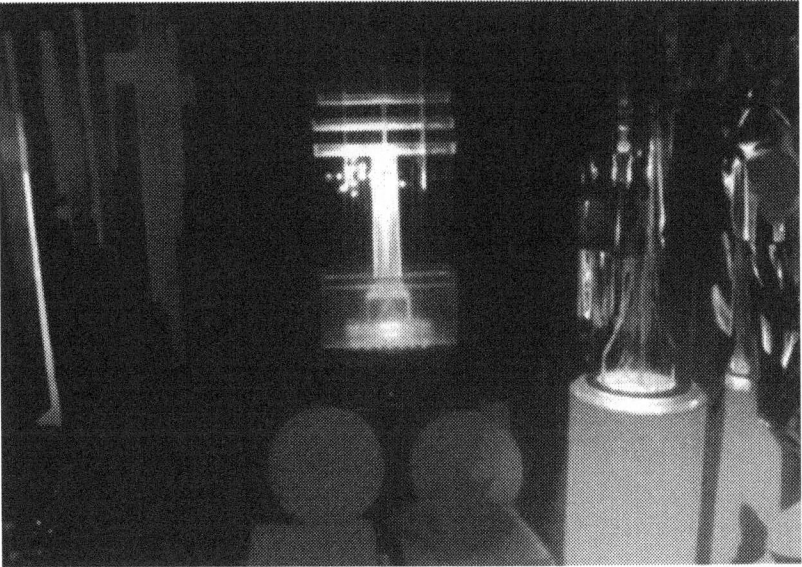

Seating in the Coconut Grive Theater.

ing recorded on tape than what would be seen during the show. "The Sun" is an integral part of the *Lumonics* theater; it is clearly a key part of the visual design.

PHASE ONE: COCONUT GROVE, 1969-1970

The initial phase of the theater lasted ten years, from 1969 until they moved it to San Diego in July 1979. This first period was marked by the construction of lighted sculptures and the invention of the name "*Lumonics*." Joseph Ardolino, the first technician to work on *Lumonics*, built controls allowing Mel's lighted sculpture to be incorporated directly into performances. These controls were installed in early 1969 enabling the theater to be born. The centralization of the lighting controls was crucial for the incorporation of the entire 355 NE 59th Terrace gallery space into the performance.

The lighted Plexiglas cubes provide the framework for the early development of *Lumonics*. Beginning in 1966, these boxes were produced and sold commercially through *Bloomingdale's* and a south Florida department store called *Jordan Marsh* as home decorations. In the 1970s, the relationship between *Lumonics* and this commercial design work was made explicit by 1973: *Grove Studios, Lumonics Design Studio*. There has been a continual movement between the commercial design work and the art produced and used in the theater.

Because the earliest theater was located in *Grove Studios*, the environment for the projections included the both commercial and fine art. They would project their visuals through and over arrangements of sculptures that would change slightly over the course of time as newer pieces were created and integrated into their studio/show room space. Animated light provided a vehicle for unifying all these separate elements with the actual space of the studio. This approach to combining different parts into a unified whole is a specific characteristic of their aesthetic through-

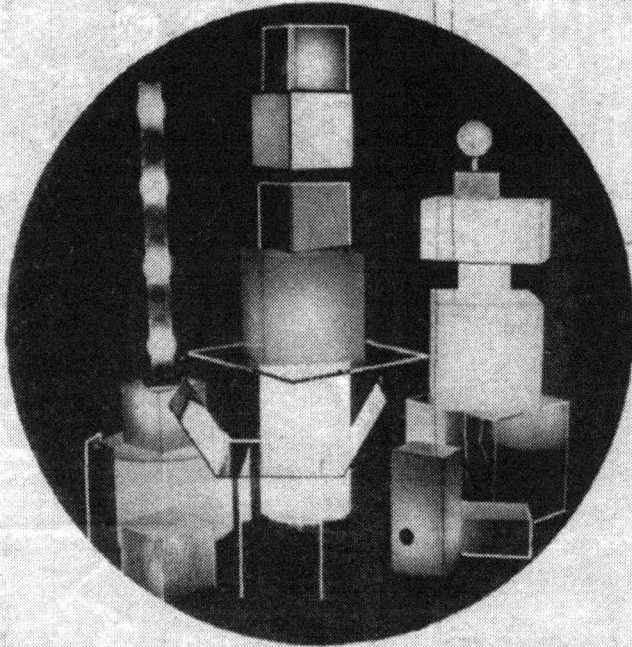

TURN IT ON!!
ENVIRONMENTAL PLEXIGLAS GALLERY

LIGHTING   SCULPTURES   WATER BEDS
WALL PIECES   FOUNTAINS   FURNITURE

FRIDAY & SATURDAY AT 9 00

LUMONIC CONCERT
A light show in the 4th DIMENSION

GROVE STUDIO

N.E. 2nd Ave.

59th St.

59th Terr.

Biscayne Blvd.

355 N E 59th Terrace

Phone 759-1312

Prices are right on

OPEN DAILY 10 30 - 5 30   Wed. eve. 8 00 - 11 00

out the history of the theater. Each *Lumonics* performance would begin with Mel and Dorothy Tanner explaining the show together for their audience seated throughout the space.

In September 1972, with their expansion into an adjoining space at 59th Terrace, the informal performances done in the studio were formalized into the first phase of the theater. These shows would last several hours, with the audience sitting on blow-up furniture, bean-bag chairs and in seats manufactured from Plexiglas specifically for use in the theater.

This theater included a series of smaller alcoves along one wall perpendicular to the projection screen. Dorothy's sculptures and fountains stood in the main floor of the room, and arranged around the walls were Mel's Plexiglas light boxes. Dorothy's works, while not containing lights themselves, would be lit with colored gels so they could reflect and refract the light passing through them, serving as vessels for bending and shaping light moving through the environment. Mel's work was solid, more lamp-like in its initial construction than Dorothy's work; consequently, it was Dorothy's sculptures that interacted directly with the projected light of the performance by standing in between the audience and the screen, while Mel's work would actively provide a lighted counterpoint to the action on screen.

These first shows used recorded music, with each section corresponding to the length of an LP, a reflection of the initial impetus behind the theater: the light shows at rock concerts. Unlike these shows which were visual decoration accompanying live music, Mel and Dorothy reversed the priorities of this type of performance by using recorded music and performing the visuals live. The first part of each show used a color organ as an overture to the main performance. Dorothy would select the music and they would take turns performing. These shows involved using color wheels, oil paint in lenses and colored liquids in trays, and slides made ahead of time and projected:

The Original Coconut Grove Theater, seen from the catwalk above the studio floor.

Mel walks over to the overheads. He pours paint into their revolving trays and turns them on. The light from underneath the overheads passes through the paint and into the beam splitters positioned above the trays. The wall fills with colored images blending, fighting, possessing each other.

The laser beam is then dropped into range and activated. A bright red dot appears on the already colored landscape. Mel plays with the lens, refracting and bending and distorting the dot to hypnotic proportions.

He then picks up a thin paint brush and walks over to the revolving pans on the overheads. He begins to paint pictures in them as the tray proceeds to revolve.[5]

This account of a *Lumonics* performance in 1975, while it incorrectly states that Mel was the main performer, when in reality both Mel and Dorothy were performing, reveals several important features of how these concerts were created, and suggests a literalization of the concept of "action painting," a school that came to dominance during the period they were in art school. The apparent movement and rotation of the visuals derives from their use of color wheels and kaleidoscopes to animate and change the color. Mel would work with the poured liquids and color wheels; Dorothy would paint in the watch glasses using a brush to directly inscribe lines into the projected light.

Each of Mel's sculptures incorporates a variety of translucent, transparent and opaque panels. His earlier abstract art anticipates his Plexiglas light boxes that contain a mixture of materials. Spray enamel layers would mask other panels tinted with *colorene*, a lighting gel produced by the theatrical lighting company Rosco. The reliefs resemble

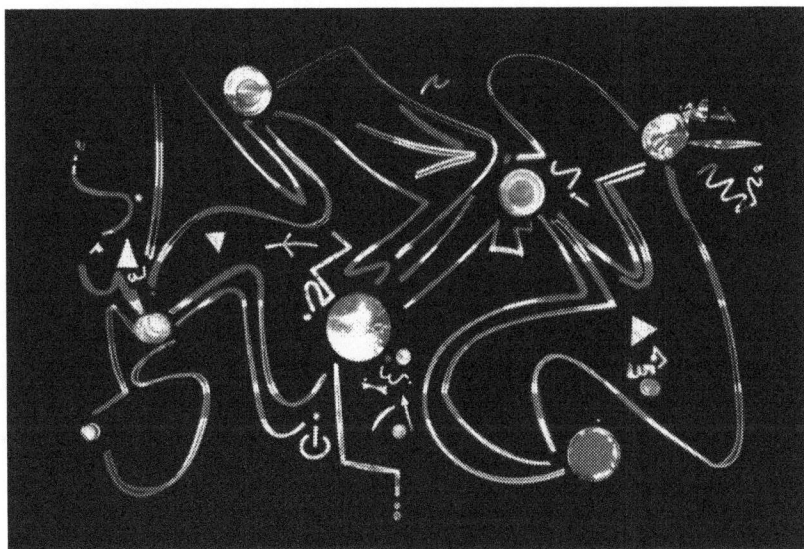

Crossroads, Mel Tanner 1974

the projections created with the overhead projectors. The inclusion of sculptures in the show served to link the projected concerts with the space of the theater in a direct way. The projected light was not an overlay on the sculpture, but was intended as a crucial component of the entire space.

While Mel's work would stand around the periphery of the space, Dorothy's transparent and translucent sculptures would stand inside the main floor of the gallery, adding a physical dimension—that of objects occupying actual space—to the graphic presence created by the patterning of Mel's work. These free standing sculptures would act to refract and contain the light from the projections, giving it a physical presence as a tangible object within the real space of the theater. Dorothy's sculptures would draw the projections off the walls and into the immediate space of the audience.

Mel's sculptures present a different series of moments from the live performance, literally—the sculptures play a role in the performances—and symbolically—the sculptures are derived from past performances. The materials chosen, primarily transparent and colored acrylic sheeting masked and linked together by opaque black, force light into being a literally physically tangible form. The structure and design of the sculptures gradually evolves from cubes mounted on rods, such as his early sculpture set "The Twelve Men," into progressively more screen-like reliefs that employ optical effects to create contrasts and the illusion of movement through interference patterns. The experience of a direct sensory encounter with the work makes a viewer aware of their own cognitive processes. In looking at these sculptures we are forced to acknowledge the partial and incomplete aspects of our own perceptions. These effects are a result of the ways that light appears through, and interacts with the sculptures themselves; their role in the concerts is a counterpoint and extension of the imagery projected on screen.

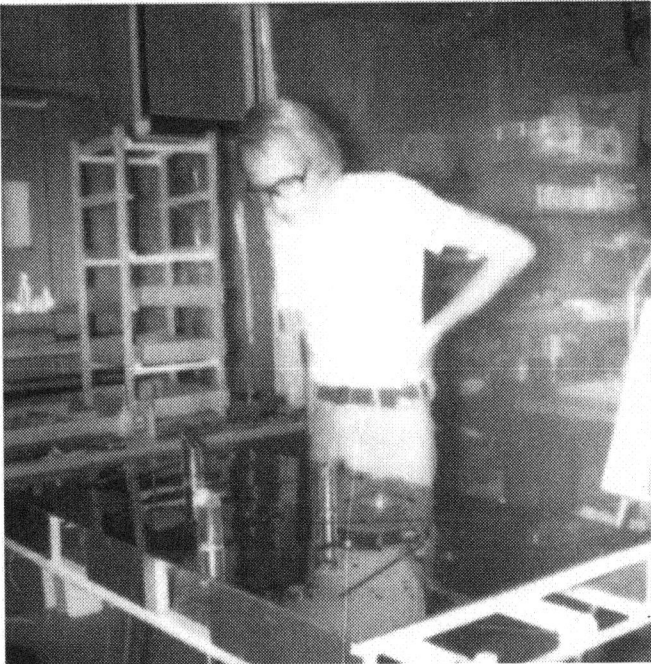

Mel Tanner at work, 1975.

PHASE TWO: SAN DIEGO, 1979-1981

Lumonics relocated to San Diego for two years, starting in 1979. This phase of the theater was secondary to a reorganization that would lead to changes in the nature and form of *Lumonics* itself. It was at this point that *Lumonics* became a collective activity based on the model of a commune or kibbutz where each member works towards a common goal. Mel and Dorothy Tanner, Mel's sister Jocelyn Tanner who was the hostess for the concerts, and their assistants Marc Billard, John Hall, Barry Raphael, Barbara Ungar, and Louise Dillon moved to San Diego with Dr. Jerry Spiegel. Dr. Spiegel had received a Federal CETA Grant to produce a series of videotapes on ecology in San Diego and brought the *Lumonics* group with him. He had come to a show and was very impressed with *Lumonics*; his involvement lasted ten years, from 1971 until 1981. While producing a series of documentaries about recycling, conservation, and ecology that were shown on cable TV, the *Lumonics* members stayed as a group in a hotel that had been moved from Rancho Santa Fe in California. They became comfortable with the arrangement and decided to maintain it; *Lumonics* became a collective endeavor.

Lumonics performances would happen once a week at their house on El Camino del Norte and, unlike the Miami theater, there was no single performance space. The sculptures were distributed throughout the parts of building that were open to the public. Instead of being theatrical, *Lumonics* in San Diego was environmental. There were two rooms for performance. One room had a video monitor, modified so that the audience would see four reflections of the screen in a mirror that extended out from the top, bottom and sides of the screen. The set itself was hidden out of sight. The other room contained kaleidoscopes and slide projects, but did not have the overheads for live performance. The shows were more concerned with synchronized light control than with the kind of live painting that defined the concerts in Miami. A third room contained a

The "California House" where performances and living space coincided.

pyramid that allowed audience members to sit and use bio-feedback equipment before and after the show.

The entrance contained a fountain, with arrangements of different sculptures spread through the rest of the rooms. This distribution of works changed *Lumonics*; the audio-visual synchronization of the lighted sculptures and the sound took precedence over the visual performances of projected light that were central to the earlier theater. It was a radical transformation that enabled them to focus more specifically on the potential of video.

Their residency in San Diego under the CETA grant created a number of television programs and allowed the *Lumonics* theater to produce its first video tape, not as a document of a live performance, but as a performance in itself. In 1978 John Hall, the electrical engineer and computer programmer who worked with *Lumonics*, purchased a video camera and began the first experiments with incorporating video into the theater; the direct result of this work was a video tape produced in 1980 and sold for home viewing.

Hall's video equipment was used to create *The Light Side of the Moon* video tape. It was the first *Lumonics* video, produced by John Hall, Mel and Dorothy. It was produced from a performance done specifically for the camera with a silver, lenticular screen. Marc build a rack specifically for the overhead projectors so they could perform in a way similar to what they had done in the earlier Miami theater. The tape they produced used Pink Floyd's *The Dark Side of the Moon* as a soundtrack. Their video experiments would not begin shaping the performances until 2000 with the transformation into a night club. Video throughout the 1980s always provided a means to promote the concerts and provided alternative ways to reach their audience.

They also experimented with bio-feedback as a way to alter perception using sets of goggled fitted with flashing leds called "synchro-energizers." These were originally part of a San Francisco hospital's program exploring bio-feedback that became a popular fad in the mid-1970s. *Lumonics* purchased several sets from Jack Schwarz and these became the focus of the "pyramid room" that contained a large arvylic smoke-colored pyramid. A limited number of audience members would be allowed to use it (due to time and space constraints) and listen to surf and winds sounds accompanied by a *Theremin*. This combination of electronic and prerecorded sounds in San Diego anticipates Marc's later combination of *Zygon* audiotapes, his own samplings and creations inspired by *Zygon*, and Dorothy's synthesizer in their music made during the 1990s.

PHASE THREE: BANGOR, 1981-1982

Lumonics third phase was conceived and built as a vehicle for *Lumonics* concerts. When their grant expired in 1981, John Hall suggested relocating to Bangor, Maine, his home town, because (he claimed) it offered good possibilities for recreating the theater as such. They converted the Canal Bank, a derelict building located at 25 Broad Street, into a performance space by blacking-in the entire interior. This performance space was the closest to a commercial theater that *Lumonics* would ever be. The transformation of the original bank into theater involved their using all the devices they had constructed for Miami and San Diego since the ground floor of their space had 3,000 square feet of performance space. The rental was exceptionally cheap, just $500.00 a month for the entire building; however, the cost of heating that space was $4,000.00 a month in winter, an expense that doomed it.

As with the earlier Miami theater, seating was low-to-the floor on pillows and seats that encouraged repose. The positioning of the audience is a key element of the *Lumonics* theater's design: instead of sitting erect in chairs, the audience is forced to sit at a much lower level, near the floor, with the seats spaced to encourage the audience to recline, viewing the performance from an almost supine position. This placement is important for the trance-state that is the goal of *Lumonics* performances. The concerts seek to alter consciousness, and the approach to this transformation is through the creation of a meditative space conducive to relaxation.

> "This is another space, not a space you
> have, that has a tendency to refresh you, to
> bring you back to yourself," [Mel] Tanner
> said.[6]

Lumonics was conceived, at least in part, as a form of civilization-therapy for people who are alienated from the world around them. The Bangor theater pursued a populist ideal for art: that it should provide an aesthetic experience for people who do not usually have access or interest in the museums. It attracted a steady audience in Bangor during the year it was located there.

> "We wanted to synthesize the idea [of
> the theater] in a downtown area where it is
> accessible to the public," [Mel] Tanner said.[7]

The issue of accessibility is connected to the issue of popularity or unpopularity, and so is a question about the audience for art. By placing the theater in a downtown space, the *Lumonics* collective made the work physically accessible to as large a public as possible. Unfortunately, while it had attracted a large enough audience to enable it to survive there, the expense of heating the building during the winters forcing them to relocate after being open for only one year to Cambridge, Massachusetts in 1982. This move forced a temporary closing of the theater while they looked for an appropriate space to install it. After three years of looking and investigating spaces that did not work out as theaters, they returned to south Florida to reopen *Lumonics* in a warehouse space Dorothy had located in Fort Lauderdale when she had been visiting her family.

PHASE FOUR: FORT LAUDERDALE, 1986-1989

The theater did not reopen in the fall of 1985 when the *Lumonics* collective returned to south Florida. In early 1986, during the period they were preparing for a new theater, a gallerist named Patricia Judith visited their Fort Lauderdale studio, looking for someone to fabricate pedestals for her gallery. While she was in their studio, she discovered the Tanner's work and became very interested in exhibiting their art at her gallery. Thus, instead of rebuilding the Lumonics theater, the first three years of their return were spent exhibiting the sculptures in a space prepared for them next-door to the *Patricia Judith Art Gallery* in Boca Raton.

This fourth phase in the evolution of the theater is an important transitional moment between the earlier theaters and the fifth phase of its existence. On October 10, 1986 a special 1,000 square foot "Lumonics Wing" was built specifically to allow the sculptures to remain on view full time as an installation whose structure and design was a combination of the Miami theater and the San Diego house. Music played while visitors walked through the space, allowing them to experience a version of *Lumonics* separate from its creator's active, immediate control. The gallery installation was closer to the work with *Hi-Fi Associates,* but was conceived as an installation rather than as an accompaniment to the music and was based around the specific aesthetics of the objects rather than their subordination to the larger theatrical concert.

Patricia Judith Fine Art presented the first exhibition of the *Lumonics* sculptures in an art gallery. The "Lumonics Wing" borrowed from all their past experiences with installing the sculptures as part of a concert. Like the Bangor theater, the entire gallery space initially had been painted black; the walls were later repainted gray to allow the sculptures greater visibility as distinct objects in themselves, while the ceiling remained black. This was the form the exhibition would retain for its entire run, and a development that would be kept for the reconstructed theater that opened in 1988.

Placing the sculptures in a gallery setting presents specific problems for the concept of Lumonics-as-theater, and reveals the extent to which the sculptures are objects independent of one another and the theater. The most significant difference between the gallery installation and the theater was the static nature of the group of pieces placed on view in the gallery. While they remained dynamic in themselves, the lights would not be animated with the same degree of synchronization that they had in the theater. Both Dorothy and Mel sold several pieces during the eighteen months the "Lumonics Wing" was open. Mel Tanner commented on the difference between the theater and the gallery installation in an interview shortly after the installation opened:

> "It [the theatrical performance] was a much more focused experience."[8]

Because the installation was an essentially static variant of the theater, animated only by the lighted sculptures themselves, and without the focus of the projections onto a proscenium screen, the gallery installation was an autonomous version of *Lumonics*. The transformation into sculpture gallery meant that the modular aspects of Mel's work would necessarily be downplayed in favor of discrete treatment as independent objects.

Live performance always incorporates a degree of audience interaction, shaping the dynamic through the feedback created by a performer's observations and responses to the audience, who respond in turn. Because of the proscenium screen, the live *Lumonics* concerts are already directed more clearly than a gallery of sculpture. By December 1986 the installation in the "*Lumonics* Wing" had evolved towards an autonomous, animated the light show,9moving the gallery away from an art installation and closer to the theater it was derived from.

Pyramid Piece, Mel Tanner 1985

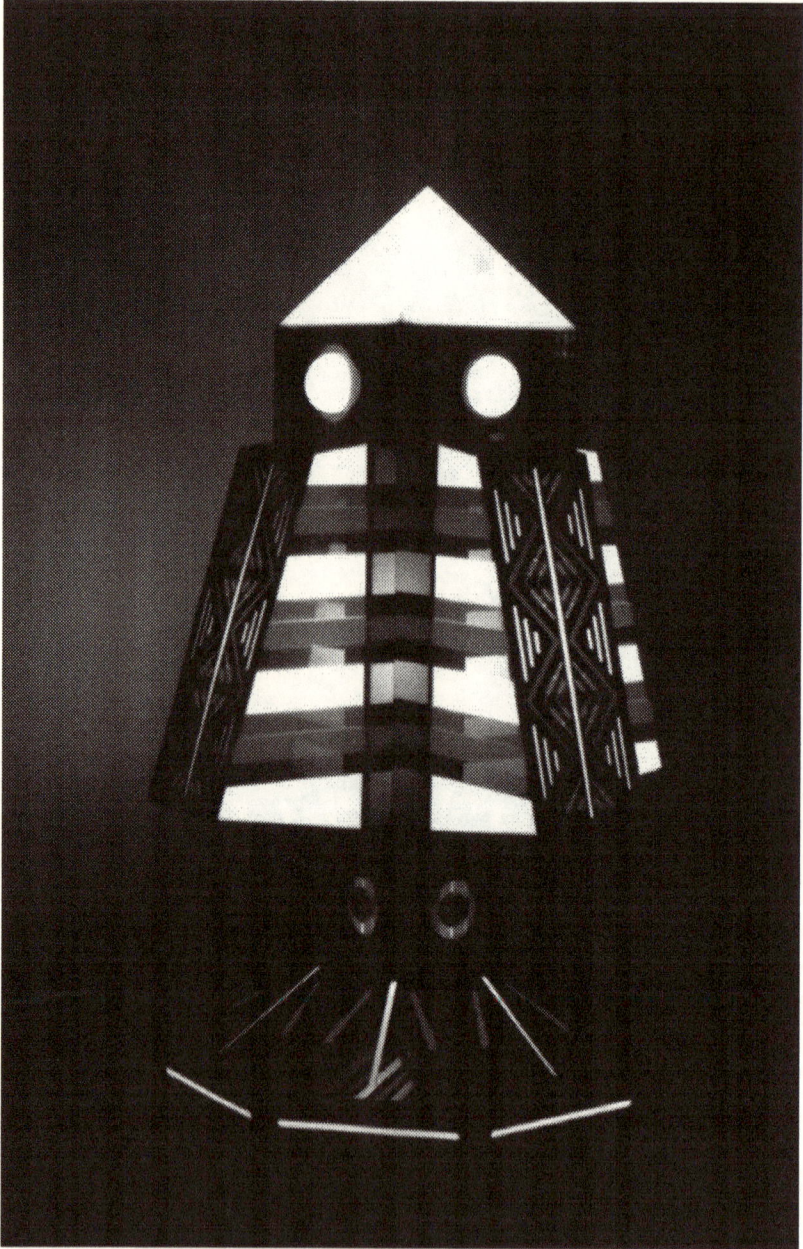

Post Egyptian, Mel Tanner 1986

Inside a Split Second, Mel Tanner 1987

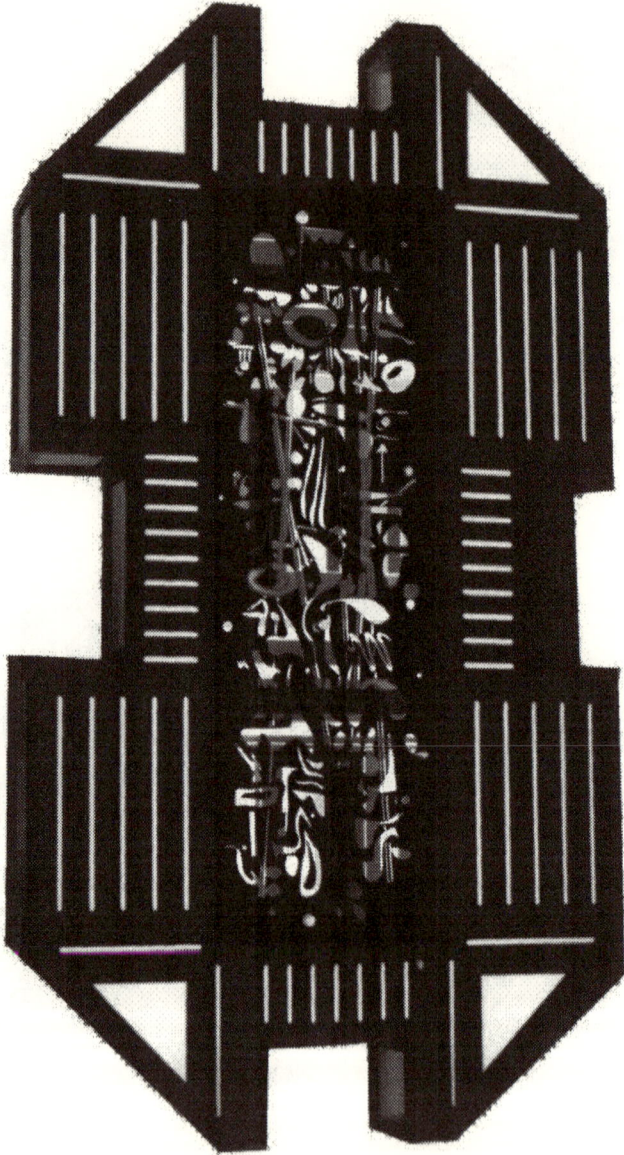

Atlantis, Mel Tanner 1986

Detail of Trans-World, Mel Tanner 1990

Number 43, Doroty Tanner, 1987

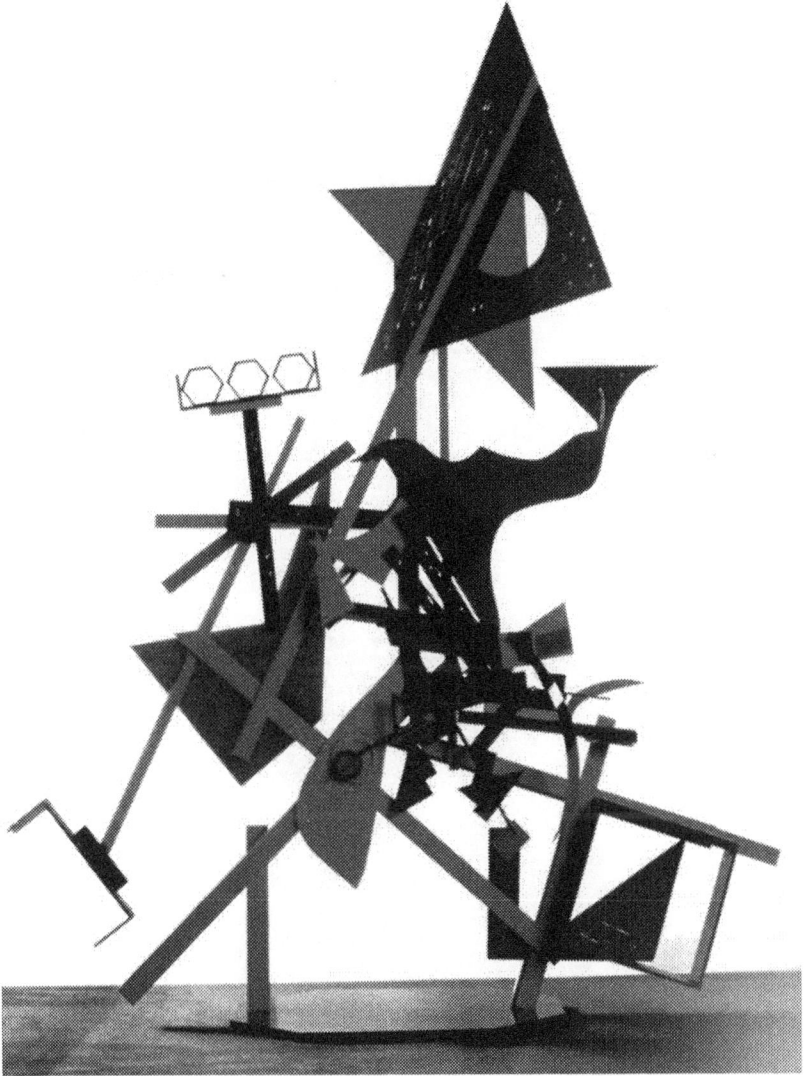

Number 48, Doroty Tanner, 1990

Number 53, Doroty Tanner, 1991

Number 58, Doroty Tanner, 1990

Rocket, Mel and Dorothy Tanner 1994

The sculptures from this period consolidate previous developments into complex, lighted screen-like panels that reflect the structure of the projected imagery in a more direct way than the lighted cubes used in the original theater. The gallery installation remained standing through the summer of 1987,10but was dismantled later that year, when *Patricia Judith Fine Art* began pressing the Tanners to sign a life-time exclusive contract with them. This contract caused the Tanners and their gallery to part ways, allowing the Tanners to reconstruct the *Lumonics* theater in their studio space in Fort Lauderdale.

PHASE FIVE: FORT LAUDERDALE, 1988-2000

The fifth phase of the theater ran from its opening in 1988 until it transformed into a dance club in October 2000. Through both phases, it was located in an office/warehouse strip mall at 3017 NW 60th Street in Fort Lauderdale, Florida. Mel Tanner died in October 1993, forcing Dorothy and Marc to continue the live performances without him. The fifth phase of the Lumonics theater, located in Fort Lauderdale, was the culmination of the collective's previous work with Lumonics, allowing them to incorporate all of their previous experiments and developments into a single work. This theater most consolidated their earlier experiments with staging, video, music and the environment into a single enveloping concert performance.

The theater was separated into three distinct rooms: an entrance dominated by the Chinese Fountain, a smaller installation room with a large television, and the main theater-gallery. The gallery recreated the proscenium screen with The Sun sculpture at the center. However, instead of being a rectangle, this screen was a white circle with a dark gray ring at its outer edge; the room was painted a lighter gray with a black ceiling, a color scheme used in the Patricia Judith Art Gallery.

In 1989 Dorothy discovered the *Zygon* company's meditation tapes that use oscillators to create different kinds of mental states in the listener. These tapes used algorithms to create their sounds, selected based upon specific psychological and physiological effects caused by listening to the soundtracks. *Zygon* exerted a direct influence on Marc's music. Until 1989 he had been creating music using a Commodore-64 computer, and developed from midi sequences of C, E and G notes that the C64 could model. Throughout the later half of the 1980s Marc worked with creating computer music , but it was not incorporated into the performances until after Mel died in 1993. The selection of music was always Dorothy's responsibility. She would occasionally use the *Zygon* tapes in the shows for transitions. These provided the initial inspiration for Marc Billard's experiments with sampling real sounds and using them to build a version of musique concrete. Marc began looking for other sources of similar kinds of rhythmic hums, similar to the kinds of sounds *Zygon* created. Marc's recordings replaced the *Zygon* tapes, and when they added Dorothy playing a synthesizer as the melody, they had their own music. Her performances on the synthesizer over what Marc was doing, created ethereal music to accompany the *Lumonics* performances.

Zygon produced its effects through a careful manipulation of low frequency (5-7 kHz) oscillator waves, but the *Zygon* tapes' effects required stereo headphones, and this was not feasible in the theater itself. The adaptation of these kinds of sounds to the theater through Marc's experiments had dramatic effects on the audience at the Lumonics concerts, and he began looking for ways to expand and reproduce these effects. His work with found sound was initially used to introduce and end sections in the performance and would occasionally be used at the end of the show as a part of their finale.

The pyramid from the "pyramid room" was installed to the right of the screen, allowing a limited number of viewers to watch the Light Side of the Moon video tape made by Mel, Dorothy and John Hall in San Diego. In 1990,

The Lumonics Theater in Fort Lauderdale.

Mel, Dorothy and Marc produced another tape, *Light Meditation* using S-VHS where they shot performances off a screen set-up specifically for viewing in the pyramid. After the concert, it would be used for biofeedback using the synchro-energizer goggles.

When the theater was reconstructed in Fort Lauderdale with the Pyramid on the right side of the screen, the synchro-energizers became a prelude to the main show. The *Nightlight Gallery*, located next-door to the main theater, was initially constructed in 1994, and the Pyramid was moved from the main theater room into that space, only to return to the theater when they changed the role of the *Nightlight Gallery* in 2000. Before the creation of the nightclub, this gallery space was used for special events following the concert. The Pyramid was removed in the beginning of 2001 because of the hazard it presented in the nightclub setting. This change marked the transition into the sixth phase of the *Lumonics* theater, that of dance club for the Rave subculture.

PHASE SIX: FORT LAUDERDALE, 2001-2003

The transformation from theater into night club happened gradually. In the period following Mel's death in 1993, Dorothy and the collective began to look at ways to expand the theater beyond the confines of a single location. It was these explorations that prepared them for the transformation into the dance club. During the "Internet rush," an investor who had made his money from the dot.com boom named Jim West, an entrepreneur, and John Fitzgerald, a filmmaker, began discussing the possible creation of a chain of five *Lumonics* theaters in London, Amsterdam, New York, Los Angeles and Rome. It was the preparations and experiments for this expansion that led to their adoption of video as a performance medium. The funding for this expansion vanished when the crash came, "wiping out" their financing for it.

The Lumonics Theater in Fort Lauderdale,
Photos by Callie Zirkle, Forum PublishingGroup, Inc.
"Eye Witness," cover story by Robin Shear, Jan. 22, 2004

The particular emphasis on live improvisation limited the potential scope of the performances; at the same time, the delicate nature of the sculptural work required for the environmental component of the theater prevented it from becoming a touring show. After Mel's death, Dorothy continued her role organizing and deciding the direction the theater should take. The movement into nightclubs began partly from economic necessity. During the period leading up to their reopening *Lumonics* itself as a nightclub, over the spand of *Lumonics'* history, the collective produced works and designs for nine night clubs around the United States and abroad, including one in Las Vegas, the *Liquid Lounge*.

Their investigations into the creation of satellite performance spaces, with the accompanying solutions to the performance issues—the adoption of prerecorded concerts and the use of video in the shows themselves—enabled the transformation from theater into night club. While in Los Angeles to prepare the designs for the first satellite theater, Dorothy noted that the "dance scene had a vitality" that interested her. John Fitzgerald had introduced them to the electronica and Rave scene during their involvement with him. Upon their return they began making changes to *Lumonics* to prepare for this new audience. This transformation marks the shift into the sixth phase of *Lumonics*. It is also the extension of their experiments at incorporating multiple arts into a singular experience. *Lumonics* reopened in October 2000 having incorporated characteristics from a dance club into its design. Dorothy's studio, located next door to the theater space, was changed to include a DJ booth, new sound system, and a dance floor. Part of this transformation was Fitzgerald's encouragement of their shift to an entirely video-based show that would allow them to expand the theater. When that proposal didn't happen, they decided to use video as a way to simplify their work loads during the concerts in the nightclub.

Performances for the Rave audience required a number of radical changes to the structure of the theater, the arrangement of sculptures on the gallery floor, and the

Theater controls in the projection booth showing light scrims and gels.

The slide carousels and overhead projectrs used in live performances.

performance. Prior to their embracing this particular audience, the people who attended the *Lumonics* concerts had
been coming for many years; the show times for the concerts were in the early evening, with the theater closing by
midnight. During the course of its involvement with Raves,
the hours gradually shifted towards later and later closing
times, and the concert that originally began the evening became the closing act, allowing the DJs, dancing, and music
to act as overture to the *Lumonics* show.

The structure of the performance also shifted over
the duration of their involvement with Raves. At first the
shows would begin at 8 p.m., but because their primary audience was interested in a venue that was open later and began later, the hours of *Lumonics* night time operation
gradually shifted to accommodate this audience. Throughout its entire history, *Lumonics* has also had a daytime program of shows for schools, and educational programs for
children. As the hours shifted later into the evening, the
volume of visitors steadily increased, forcing a rearrange-
ment of the theater for the safety of both sculpture and audience alike. Dorothy's free-standing, angular sculptures
had to be moved onto elevated platforms or placed in stor-
age, and the fountain that stood in the entrance area was removed and replaced by a box office style counter. These
logistical changes also meant a change in aesthetics away
from the meditative, relaxed *Lumonics* concerts towards the
more active, beat-oriented dance music that characterized
electronica.

Dorothy and Marc collaborated on the creation of
the videos used in these performances, drawing on their
older recordings initially made with S-VHS in the early
1990s with Mel, then later using digital programs like *Abode
AfterEffects* and *Premiere* to generate new material still
rooted in the aesthetic of the earlier live performances. For
the shows they would rely primarily on the video, but
would incorporate live performance into it as a way of
breaking up the video in improvisational ways that the digital technology would not. The fusion of these two antithet-
ical processes resulted in the specific character of the

concerts during this phase and allowed them to begin producing videotapes and DVDs for educational purposes as
well as sell tapes to their younger audience during their run
as a nightclub.

The abstract character of the *Lumonics* performances
was accentuated by using video because they were no longer constrained to those effects that could be produced
manually. Dorothy felt that the videos allowed them to create a stronger version of the show, especially since they
could still incorporate live elements into the show:

> "The fact that it is all abstract allows people to
> disassociate, particularly with the video. You can
> see it one way or another—it has no purpose
> except as a visual experience. We're trying to
> liberate you from how you usually think."
> [Dorothy]

The utopian belief in the power of art as a transformative
force is crucial to understanding the consistency of
Lumonics as an aesthetic system over its entire history. This
is a view of art that regards it as a therapy, and it is this ability to change consciousness and understanding that shapes
all aspects of the videos' form. The duration, rhythm and
repetition employed in the creation of these videos mirrors
the repetitive structure of the *Zygon* audio—the oscillations
serve to produce meditative, relaxing mental states in the
audience. This kind of repose marks the distinction between earlier avant-garde theater, other abstract video and
film work and *Lumonics,* and connects it to the historical im-
perative of American museal culture, to uplift, educate and
enlighten.[11]

These later videos, as with the earlier ones, proceed
as an encapsulated form of the live, improvisational show,
modified and condensed for viewing on a video monitor.
Their use of digital video is as a way to recreate the kinds of
effects formerly produced with colored liquids in the overheads. The oscillations created by physical waves become
the patterns produced by digital simulations of oscillators;
the interference patterns produced through contrasting

The front wall (screen) of the Fort Lauderdale Theater during a performance..

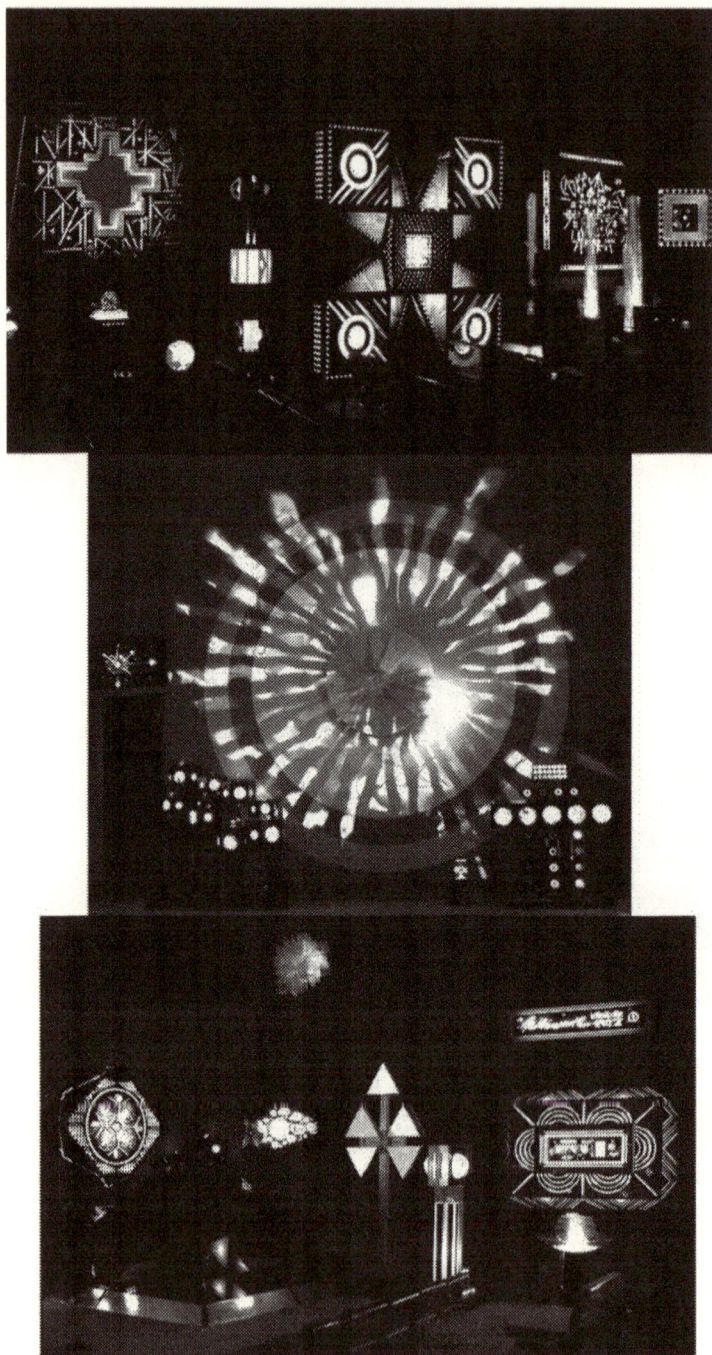

Left, Front (screen) and Right walls of theater

light and incompatible pigments are reproduced thorough masks and filters in *AfterEffects*. The result is a reproducible kind of theater where different parts of the performance can be work and reworked over a long period of time, allowing Dorothy and Marc a greater degree of latitude in the kinds of shows they can produce. It also simplified the logistics for the concerts during the run of the nightclub.

With the transformation of Dorothy's studio space located adjacent to the theater into the *Nightlight Gallery* in 2000, *Lumonics* formalized the arrangements that had existed informally. With the addition of the dance floor in the center of the gallery, *Lumonics* was ready to expand its audience through a transformation from being a theater into being a nightclub. This was a gradual shift, coming as the younger audience for their shows began to grow. They had not expected this audience; the audience they had been looking for was "an older crowd," that was interested in New Age experimentation. The first DJ they hired, Drew Bongiorno, reflected this interest, and it was not until their New Year's Eve show in 2000/2001 that younger audience began showing up in large numbers.

Initially they worried about the generational difference with the new audience that was more than twenty years younger than the collective, but they discovered that this was not an issue. Dorothy noted that "they were receptive to what we threw at them." Barry Raphael became responsible for the promotion through the website and over the internet, gradually building their audience, with the result that they were soon (and for the first time) making a large profit on the *Lumonics* theater itself.

However, there were problems with this audience, the most prominent being that of the illegal drug, Ecstasy. There is a continuous history of police interest and response to theaters of this type once they reach a certain level of visibility. *Lumonics* encountered the *Rave Task Force,* created after the Fort Lauderdale Police Department received funding for a grant called Project Ecstasy on October 1, 2001. The *Lumonics Light and Sound Theatre* was the first rave club closed by the task force. They raided *Lumonics* on

May 24, 2002, arrested five audience members, and forced them to close because code enforcement officers found multiple fire, building, and zoning violations and closed the club.12The theater had been built without getting the proper construction permits or inspections. This raid marked the end of the theater. By 2005 it had been disassembled, and Lumonics had vacated the space.

Back Wall of Theater; entrance is to the left of the frame.

NOTES

[1] Robbins, Dave. "World's First Review of a Lumonics Concert," in *Mensanity*, n.d. (prior to September 18, 1970).

[2] Gillmon, Rita. "What is Lumonics?," in *The San Diego Union*, September 19, 1980, B1.

[3] Warm, David. *XS Magazine*, July 9-15, 1996, np.

[4] Marlowe, John. "Lumonics It's 2,000 light years from home" in *The Miami News*, May 16, 1975, p.3

[5] Marlowe, p. 3.

[6] Grosswiler, Paul. "Sculpture fuses light and sound," in *Bangor Daily News, Maine Event* supplement vol. VII, no. 37, March 20-21, 1982, p. ME 3.

[7] Grosswiler, p. ME 3.

[8] Boccio, Rose. "'Mermerizing' art form lights up Boca gallery" in *The Sun-Sentinel*, November 6, 1986, p. 8.

[9] Sheffied, Skip. "Exhibit Glows in the dark at Boca," in *The Boca Raton News*, December 15, 1986, np.

[10] Photographs of the works were featured in *The Palm Beach Post,* in a special section on the art galleries in Boca Raton that were staying open for the summer. *TIFG,* "Shining On," June 5, 1987, pp. 24-26.

[11] Munson, Lynne. *Exhibitionism (Chicago: Ivan R Dee, 2000), pp. 132-152.*

[12] DeMarzo, Wanda. "Rave Club Closed by New Drug Task Force," in *The Miami Herald*, Broward Section, May 31, 2002, p. 5B.

AUTOBIOGRAPHIES

Mandarin 1, Mel and Dorothy Tanner 1985

DOROTHY TANNER

FROM THE BEGINNING

I met Mel Tanner in 1950. A mutual friend and fellow student at the Brooklyn Museum Art School wanted me see his work. The studio was in the basement of a private house. A slim, dark haired, very serious looking person greeted us at the door. After a brief introduction, Mel led us into his studio. I was amazed by what I saw.

The paintings were sweeping non-objective color studies, the technique was somewhere between Suerat and Van Gogh. He had applied the paint with small brush strokes and palette knife to build overlays of color, using a wax medium to achieve a rich but controlled texture. They were beautiful, professional looking finished art pieces, certainly not the work of a student...

That night we argued about politics (I was somewhat more radical than he) but essentially we were both anti-establishment.

After knowing one another for about nine months, we were married in July 1951. The installation of a pre-fab, metal shower made the studio livable. The garage behind the house became my studio.

I have since seen Mel and I as "old souls" that had agreed somewhere else to hook up again in this lifetime, to see what trouble or fun we could get into together, this time around . . .

In 1952, Mel's G.I. benefits ran out. My unemployment checks stopped. We took part-time jobs in Manhattan . . . Part-time jobs paid very little, traveling back and forth from Brooklyn took a lot of time, leaving very little time for anything else. When my former employer offered me a job managing a store in Syracuse at a salary that was double what we'd been earning, it was easy to say yes...especially since it would give us more control of our time as well as better studios and living quarters . . ..

Leaving NY was the downside . . . but having a car would enable us to drive into the city as often as we wanted.

1952-1963 SYRACUSE

The house in Syracuse was a two-story building with a "carriage house" that became my studio. Mel's studio occupied the front of the house . . . it was a comfortable arrangement . . .

The "carriage house" was large enough for me to cast in plaster, build large metal sculptures, and experiment with polyester as a medium. Although I continued to do portraiture in wood and clay for a few years, the freedom that was possible with welding metal and polyester constructions dominated my interest . . .I was challenged with making the medium of sculpture a totally spontaneous expression.

Mel's work became radically different from the "pointillist" color studies he had done in Brooklyn. Those early paintings took months of painstaking application to complete . . . .. Changing his medium from oil and wax to acrylics allowed him more direct expression. After a series of small free form lyrical canvasses, he settled into explorations combining calligraphy with geometric shapes. It was very productive period.

In 1959 we decided to convert the second floor of our house into an Art School. We gave classes in painting and sculpture. It was an interesting occupation for a while, but we had come to the realization that it was time to go back to New York.

In 1962 we placed an ad in the *New York Times* for artists that wanted to be represented in a New York gallery. It would be a cooperative, with Mel and I selecting the artists and curating the shows. The response was overwhelming.

We found a gallery on E. 57 St., between Park and Madison Ave. It was a prime location, yet affordable. We packed up and moved into a loft on E. 29 St. where we could live and have studios.

NEW YORK

We opened the gallery 1963. The Armond Hammer gallery was on the ground floor, ACA above it, and our Granite Gallery on the third. It was a small gallery but the location was important and attractive to the diverse group of New York and out-of town artists that joined us and helped to support it.

The art scene in New York was in turmoil. Abstract expressionism was in the late days of its heyday. Op and pop art were coming up strong, and minimalism was just around the corner.

By 1965 the challenge of operating a gallery in the heart of NY's most prestigious art district, the excitement, the glitz, the glamour began to wear thin. Socializing, courting clients, meeting the "right people" . . . it just was not our thing. Essentially we refused to do what it takes to "make it. "

The Gallery was sufficiently respected to garner a few reviews by *New York Times* art critic Brian O'Dougherty. No small thing in the light of the number of important galleries on the street that *The Times* did not review.

After two years of living a schizophrenic life of gallery owner by day and artist by night, we closed the gallery and our studio on E. 29th St. and left New York in Sept. 1965. Boarded a freighter out of Tampa, bound for Rotterdam, perhaps to find another life in Europe . . . traveling Europe in a feisty little blue VW was a blast, but we soon realized that living there was not really an option. It wasn't what we were looking for.

We returned from Europe in the fall of 1967, out of money and clueless as to where to go. In many respects we were more like the kids that we met roaming about in Europe than our contemporaries. We stopped in Miami to visit my parents before heading out for the west coast, deciding to rest there for a while first. Twelve years later we were still there.

Coincidently, Miami had become a destination for young people that were hitting the road. They were coming from all over the country, some remained, others were using Miami as a jumping off point for parts unknown...the counter culture was in full bloom.

The Vietnam War had already radicalized large segments of the youth. There was a social revolution going on and music had become the universal conduit for protest. Large numbers of people were backpacking it, doing psychedelics, searching for more meaningful lives. Black Power . . . Women's Lib...Civil Rights...and lots of hippies.

MIAMI

Miami was called the "the Magic City" then. It was a place of magic for the both of us. I use the word magic here to describe a spiritual experience that defies logical explanation. Yes, there was a "beam of light" that glanced off the wing of a plane flying overhead. Mel was struck by the light and was forever changed. This was more than an

Dorothy Tanner, 1968.

out-of-body experience. It yielded a more profound view of life, and instruction as to how to realize it more fully. That was in the summer of 1969.

Previous to Mel's "experience" we had built a business around a material that we encountered while we still had the gallery in NY. The material was plexiglas. Taken with its light transmitting qualities and color, we produced functional products that were aesthetically satisfying and saleable as well. These were cubes and pedestals that "contained light." It was a new idea and it clicked, providing us with needed income and gave us the time to produce art with a new exciting material.

After Mel's experience, building light sculptures became the major focus. We converted the studio into a theatre and acquired the technology, "a color organ," that made it possible to synchronize the light sculptures with music. The control panel was set up by Joe Ardilino to handle slide projectors, overhead projectors, and the color organ. Fred Torchio and Bill Borkan helped us put our quadraphonic sound system together. We laid carpet, bought blow-up furniture and waterbeds, freaked everything out with mylar . . . we were ready to do light shows.

These were Light Shows like no other . . . at the end of a street of funky warehouses and shabby residences, on the corner of 59th Terrace across from the railroad tracks, stood the Theatre. The impact of walking into another world, beautiful, strange yet familiar was tremendous. For some it was like returning home, and they didn't want to leave.

On Saturday night people would arrive about 9:30 they were in their late teens and early 20's. They would "hang out," some talking quietly, others sitting staring at the pieces silently tripping out. From our perch on the mezzanine we began the concert. The music could be Moody Blues, Pink Floyd, or a host of other sound that gave voice to the complaints and aspirations of that generation.

People told us of their experiences during the shows and how they felt afterward. We heard about out-of-body trips, seeing people that had died, problems solved, doing

Mel Tanner, 1975.

better on school exams, physical healings. Life changing experiences...it was all pretty heady stuff.

The years from 1969 to 1978 saw the neglect of our "business." However, through the efforts of Jocelyn and Louise, some designers became aware of our studio and we received commissions as a result. Barry, Marc and Barbara joined us in 1972.

We did special performances for a variety of groups along with our regular Saturday night concerts. new techniques were developed. A friend, videographer John Hall, made it possible for us to experiment with bringing abstract visuals and music to VHS videotapes.

FLORIDA 1978

When one of our window air-conditioners was stolen, along with a newly planted Yucca tree, the message to move came in loud and clear . . . The neighborhood had become dangerous . . . time to leave . . . .

Coincidently, our friend Jerry Spiegel who was then living in California was awarded a CETA grant. We were commissioned by him to produce a videotape pertaining to ecology. The visuals were semi-abstract; the music included "In the Eyes of a Child" by Moody Blues.

CALIFORNIA 1979

Mel and I flew to CA. to prepare the small Honeymoon hotel that was made available to us. The "hotel" was set in the hills of North County, about 20 miles north of San Diego. It needed repair. There was a kidney shaped pool that was surrounded by large trees and fragrant vines, bougainvillea, roses, and birds of paradise. It also had another structure on the property that became a video studio.

With the help of Jerry Spiegel and some of his friends from a commune located in Dulzura, south of San

Diego. The place was made ready to receive the Lumonics crew from Miami . . . In the large central room; sculptures were set up and wired for color organ, kaleidoscopes, slide projectors and a sound system. The fireplace wall was draped with fabric, and a pyramid shaped sculpture came out of the hearth. This was the performance space. We treated each of the three hotel "suites" as intimate environments that held wall and freestanding sculptures. One housed the plex pyramid that we brought with us; another had a television monitor that showed the video that we produced. We invited people into the "Lumonics" house that we lived in.

A feature article in the *San Diego Union*, and word of mouth brought people to this hard to find place in Olivenhain on Saturday nights. After 2 years the property was sold. We had to move.

MAINE 1981

John Hall who had come with us from Miami offered us his house in Old Town Maine. We needed a place to go. Everything was packed into a couple of semis that we drove across country. We lived in John's house and leased a four-story bank building in Bangor a few miles from Old Town. We painted the windows black, constructed a wall to conceal the bank vault, that also to served as a projection screen; installed our sound system, and let it be known that we were open to the public. We created a very elegant, finished looking space.

The *Bangor Daily News*, *The Weekly Journal*, and an alternative publication, *Sweet Potato* gave us great reviews and people came. Although we attracted the sophisticated people of the town, and sold some work, there was no way we could survive financially. While the building rent was only $500 a month, the heating bill was in the thousands. Winter nights in Maine go to 20 below zero. Nine months after our arrival, we were on our way to Boston.

In 1981, perhaps the most notable piece of art that we produced in Maine with John Hall was a video to the music of Carl Orff's "Carmina Burana."

BOSTON 1982—85

Strapped for funds when we arrived in Boston in the spring of 1982, we settled for a small studio with a large basement in which we stored all of the theatre gear that was left in crates. We lived in Cambridge . . . . Everyone except for Mel, Marc, and I got jobs. Mel and I looked for plex fabrication work to support the studio.

We were commissioned to design the set for public television station WGBH's "Frontline," and a world map for WBZ-TV, and custom work for the Boston Museum of Science.

I began to use the oven to bend plex and constructed a number of freestanding sculptures. Our engineer John Hall remained in Maine, so Marc began to teach himself electronics. Mel reworked some of his earlier pieces.

In 1984, I was ill with an ulcer. After a hospital episode, rest and sunshine was the recommendation. Two weeks in Florida would help me to recuperate. In March of 1985, we stayed at a motel on the beach in Fort Lauderdale. A few days after our arrival, we made the decision to move back to Florida. After 9 months in Maine and 3 years in Boston, going back to Florida felt good. In one week, we located a warehouse and a place to live.

We left Boston on April Fool's Day with wet snow falling on the windshields . . . on the road heading south . . . it was like going home.

FORT LAUDERDALE 1985

The warehouse we occupied was ideal. Like the one in Miami, it had a mezzanine, but it was larger, the ceilings

Jocelyn Tanner, 1985.

were higher, on a nice street, in an attractive Spanish style building that was well maintained.

When the owners of a Boca Raton gallery came looking for display pedestals and saw the work we were doing, they offered us representation. They leased a 1500 square foot space adjoining their gallery to house our work. It was the Lumonics wing of the Patricia Judith Gallery. The addition of my free-form sculptures that were externally lighted served as a compliment to Mel's geometric lighted wall pieces. The installation was very well received by the critics, and sales were good . . . when the owners asked us to sign what was practically a lifetime contract, we refused. After a year and a half with the Gallery it was time to build the Theatre again. What better place to do it than the studio we were in.

We were inspired once again by the idea that we would be creating a non-verbal, sensory, healing, transforming experience that would be of benefit to anyone that could get there. Not just for those who could afford to own the art. It would have been practical to ride the success we had with selling art and furthering our careers as artists, but the event that altered our lives in 1969, Mel's spiritual peak experience, required something more of us: to build another theatre.

FORT LAUDERDALE 1987

We constructed a wall to separate the studio shop from the performance space. It also served as our projection screen. The mezzanine had the rudiments of a control booth. We set up projectors, kaleidoscopes, the laser etc. Mel and I created large sculptures to further enhance the space. Marc installed the sound system, and by the spring of 1988, The Lumonics Light and Sound Theatre opened to the public . . . on Friday and Saturday nights. Our audiences were people of all ages and stripes. The music was high energy electronic, and almost always included one classical piece . . . .

In 1989, we were ending the concerts with 20 minutes of low frequency sound, along with our visuals, bringing the audiences into a very high meditative state. The large plex pyramid was made available for people to experience the synchro-energizer—a biofeedback device that Barbara manipulated. We were attracting the "New Agers."

Mel died in 1993, after a very short illness. I was faced with the question of my willingness, as well as my ability to continue the theatre without him . . . I believed that what I had been dedicated to for so many years was still valid and worth doing. The people that we shared our lives with wanted to continue to keep the idea alive. Fortunately, Marc who was involved in every aspect of the work was there to assist me in any way that he could. After several months we reopened the theatre.

Marc had shown an early interest in computers. In 1986 we acquired a Commodore 64, and shortly thereafter we bought our first synthesizer, a Cassio CZ-101. The digital age had begun for us...Marc experimented with low frequency sound, and composed a few pieces of music that we used for our 20-minute meditations in the theatre. I began to use the synthesizer and together we collaborated to compose music. We produced cassettes that were sold in the Theatre and Borders Books.

In 1994 we extended the gallery into a portion of the studio that I had shared with Mel. His wall pieces and my sculptures (work that had not been seen before) comprised the environment for the "Drum-Dance Theatre." We invited the drummer "Hodeen" to facilitate the drumming. We had a Mayan night, with a shaman, an African night with a dancer and drummer from Senegal. There were a host of interesting events in which we blended the talent with our performance in the theatre. The additional space allowed for greater interaction and audience participation. Marc and I continued to work together creating music, video and sculpture.

FORT LAUDERDALE 1999

John Fitzgerald had come to the theatre for years before he introduced himself and his friend, Jim West. Jim fell in love with Lumonics and invited us to L.A. He owned a building there that he hoped would be suitable for a Lumonics nightclub. We were to design a pilot. His projection was to form a public corporation to finance four more venues. New York, London, Amsterdam and Rome.

We were flown to L.A. and after we approved the building, Jim hired a videographer to work on a documentary about Lumonics. In the following month the videographer Oleg arrived in Ft. Lauderdale to assemble material for his documentary.

The year 2000 was the year the stock market went south...venture capital dried up. Jim was an entrepreneur. The project was kaput . . .

After taking a few months to recuperate, we decided to do the club on our own, without backing . . . a nightclub that did not serve alcohol.

The rave scene was going full tilt. *PLUR:* peace, love unity, respect. The similarities of these young people with those of the 60s and 70s were unmistakable. It spoke of a sentiment that was easy for us to relate to.

Once again music was the conduit for protest and change, and dancing was an integral part of it. My long-held desire to see dancing a part of the Lumonics experience could now be realized.

Designing the space for dance parties went easily. My sculpture was removed from the floor and placed on high platforms. Mel's work was arranged high on the walls, protection for the art and the people. Marc built the dj booth and sturdy seating that Barbara covered with soft synthetic fur. He installed the lighting and the sound system. Everyone helped . . . it was a labor of love . . . I had the job of booking the djs, planning the line-up, getting flyers printed and distributed, etc.

We were about to learn to connect with a new generation of people that we had little previous contact with. I was as interested in them as they were curious about all of us. After all, I was old enough to be their grandmother and the rest of us could have been their parents . . . but it worked. It took 6 months to get the word out . . . . After a year we were operating Friday and Saturday night and getting crowded. Too crowded.

On May 25, 2002 shortly after midnight we were raided. The police with dogs in tow proceeded to search the people. The new federally funded Rave Task Force "Project Ecstasy" entered illegally. There was no warrant. The police report that was filed shamelessly falsified information that was published in the newspapers. We were cited for code violations. The violations had to do with work done without applying for permits.

DECEMBER 2004

Our attempts to comply with the code violation charges proved to be too expensive. Also, despite the fact that we had obtained a variance for assembly in 1988 we were told that changes in zoning regulations would no longer honor the variance. In short, we would not be allowed to continue with the theatre at that location.

We continued to receive email and phone calls. I'm touched by the love that was engendered by the dance party events. The powerful vibration of the art along with the effect of the concert on the dance party people proved Lumonics to be a vehicle for transport once again, as it has been in the past.

I have come to think of Lumonics as a space ship that has traversed many lifetimes, many universes, and is now moored in Fort Lauderdale, awaiting its next assignment. Its first captain has gone on to other realms and left the vessel in the care of his first mate and loyal crew.

Photos by Callie Zirkle, Forum Publishing Group, Inc.
"Eye Witness," cover story by Robin Shear, Jan. 22, 2004

THE CREW

In 1972, a bearded, longhaired young schoolteacher from Chicago showed up. Barry Raphael had quit his job and decided to join us. Since then he has demonstrated again and again his dedication, and unfailing optimism. He has provided the quality fuel necessary to help keep the vessel intact.

Later in the same year Marc Billard made his appearance. He had experience in carpentry and a great desire to connect with us. His ready ability to work with plexiglas made it possible for Mel to design more expansively, and design he did. Since Mel's demise, he has become a co-creator in all things Lumonics. I am particularly grateful to him for making it possible by way of his electronic expertise for me to pursue my first love ... music ....

I view Barbara Ungar as a personal gift.... she was Marc's friend and quickly became mine. Early on, she assumed responsibility for whatever had to be done, from working with Marc in the shop fabricating plex, to making the clothing that we wore. Most important, are her psychic gifts that helped to inform some of my most difficult decisions.

Ritch Mosias is a relatively new crew member (1995). His drumming talents, as well as his natural ability to connect with children insured the success of the special daytime performances. He brought some children forward to drum with him, others drummed sitting in their seats, while some children just got up and danced. It was delightful to see the whole room literally jumping for joy, particularly when it involved physically and mentally challenged children.

Mel's sister Jocelyn played hostess for us in Miami. She was made for the job. People loved her. She was charming, and had the family's grace and refined good looks. Mel was her younger brother, and she was there to do battle with her father when Mel decided he was going to make Art his life. Jocelyn was very much a part of our lives throughout ... she died in 1985 ....

Barbara Unger and Rich Mosias, 2003.

Louise Dillon was Jocelyn's friend, the daughter of the Superintendent of the New York State Troopers. Surprisingly she had little of the up-tightness you might expect, given her conventional background. As a grade school teacher in Miami, she arranged to bring her fifth grade students to Lumonics with the objective of increasing their creative writing skills.

Jerry Spiegel would have become a member of the crew had he not been the father of three children and responsible for their care. One of his ideas was to have his clients experience Lumonics before a counseling session with him. As a professional teacher and counselor he believes that the Lumonics environment induces a state of well being and awareness that accelerates the learning process.

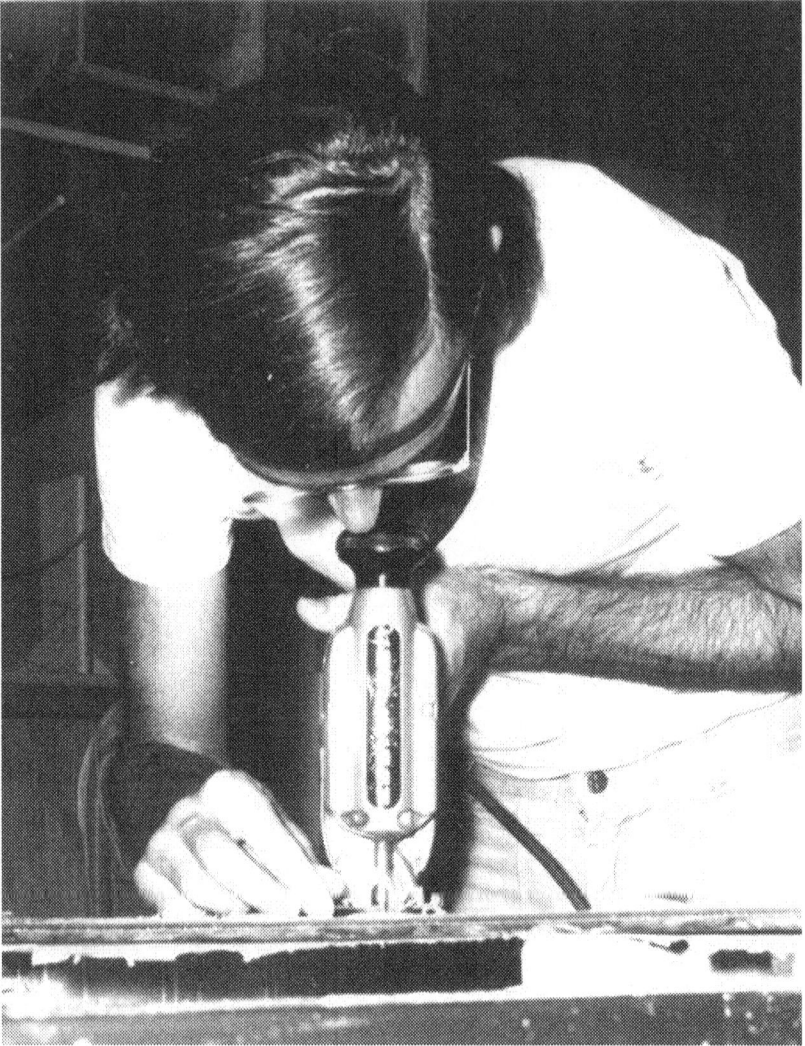

Marc Billard working on one of Mel's pieces, 1996.

MARC BILLARD

It was a hot night in Miami in 1972. I had an address from a lady (Mel's sister Jocelyn) who had lived next door to me the year before. She had said her brother was doing something rather fantastic at this address. The note was faded and almost unreadable a year later when it occurred to me to go there. It was a time in my life when I was really looking for something meaningful to be involved in. Somehow I found my way to the address and Mel, Dorothy, Jocelyn, and a few others were hanging out in their theater.

The environment wasn't like anything I had seen before except for a "daydream" I had experienced 5 years previous about a room full of colored lights. I was speechless until it was time to go when Mel asked me what I did for a living. I was a rough carpenter at the time and Mel said he could use some of that kind of labor. I started to show up at their studio next door 2-3 times a week, gratis after work. There was some shop infrastructure and saw tables to build.

At that time Mel and Dorothy were working with an old craftsman - Pete - who showed me how to work with Plexiglas. It was an unbelievably quick learn for me, (I had never thought of myself as a craftsman), like I had been doing it for years. After 3 months of gratis work they asked me to work full time.

The work varied from wall pieces to freestanding sculpture to work for designers and architects with a few lighted dance floors, lighted ceilings, and wall sculptures thrown in. The theater and gallery were being constantly transformed by the new work. A 9' plush pyramid was constructed for the gallery with a sound system, synchro-energizer, a theramin, and a ventilation system. The gallery windows by that time were all fitted with Lumonics "stained glass" art.

The Saturday night performances were the highlight of the week, starting at 10 PM and lasting 2 hours or so. You had to pour a lot of the people out the door after an experience that powerful, back into a slightly funky warehouse district late at night.

Around 1974, I started to build light projection devices for the theater, color wheels, Plexiglas lenses and beam splitters, turning trays for the overhead projectors, modifying spotlights, and experimenting with everything I could think of. I studied optics a little, but hands on trial/error experimentation was much more satisfying.

In 1979, we moved to the North County San Diego area and set up a theater with less projection possibilities in a hotel that had been moved and turned into a residence. Most people had to travel 20-40 miles to get there. It was quite successful for the location.

Mel worked on a few of his older works doing some very delicate rehabs. For the next 2 years we built wall pieces and fountains for showrooms in Beverly Hills and Los Angeles. A video for a government CETA grant was produced in the "garage" that had been turned into a video studio.

In 1981, we moved to Bangor, Maine and setup a full-blown theater (minus the overhead projectors) in a 12,000 square foot bank building. Our engineer John Hall bought a full 3/4" UMatic studio and we produced our first videos.

We were way up in the north woods of Maine and Plexiglas had to be shipped from New Hampshire. The building had no elevator and the shop was on the third floor and it was difficult to work on the art form - we were in and out of there in 9 months.

In 1982 we moved to Boston with very few financial resources. Within 8 months we had a very successful bulk food bin fabrication business with all the Lumonics crew working part of the operation. Mel and Dorothy did the packing. The fabrication business was interesting for a year and a half but wore a little thin emotionally.

Mel started to work, again reworking some of his older sculptures. Dorothy started to work for the first time in 15 years doing free-form floor and table sculptures. It was also time for something else. We approached the architects rehabbing Horticultural Hall in Boston, but the fit of a nighttime venue and proper access to the space that was possible for us didn't gel. We also picked up an account with a lady whose interest was in creating custom furniture and lamps that I describe as somewhere between art and architecture.

In this period I got interested in electronics and started to study. I also set up our projection system in the cellar of our house and learned how to setup run, and maintain it. We had previously had engineers coming around to help with the electronics, but I felt we needed to be able to do it ourselves. I also start to listen to all the albums we had in our collection - 100's of them and set up a small recording setup with what little equipment we had.

In 1985 we moved to Ft. Lauderdale. It was a totally different business environment, especially for plexiglas. There wasn't a living possible for us in it. The designers we contacted in South Florida somehow could not see the artwork. The art/architecture lady contacted us after 8 months in Ft. Lauderdale and I continued working for her 2-3 months or so of the year for the next 10 years, providing some needed financial stability. It was the type of work that only I could do with a little help from Barbara.

Mel's' work was getting larger. Dorothy really picked up pace and they were both creating a lot of work, some of it rather solid (my insistence on strength and longevity), and large. In 1986 we were represented in a gallery in Boca Raton for 1 1/2 years selling quite a few works. An insistence by the gallery owners on a long-term contract on "their terms" blew us out of the gallery situation.

Starting in 1986 my quest for my own place in the art form started to come to the fore. I didn't know if I could really produce anything on my own, but I had to try. First we bought a computer, then midi software and a synthesizer. I started to construct a music studio building mixers and processors from scratch, burning and wiring the circuit boards. The idea that you could use your imagination to create music/sound without spending years learning how to play instrument was fascinating.

In1988 it was time to do the theater again. I was now prepared (in an engineering sense) to set up the whole thing by myself. I rehabbed the electronics panel and electrical distribution system and put together a high quality sound system. We put an ad in the main Ft. Lauderdale paper, got a hundred reservations and were shut down before our first show by the building department for running a theater in a warehouse district (zoning). Mel and Dorothy went down to the zoning board and on second attempt got a zoning variance for the theater. It was a much slower start after that and it took 6-8 months of small audiences to really get up and running. We then started to pick up some press and the audiences grew to an acceptable level.

The really theater took off for a couple of years with the New Age crowd in 1990 -1992. The theater setup was pretty refined by that time.

In 1990 affordable SVHS equipment came out on the market. We picked up a camera, video deck, and video processor, and started shooting again. Only one videotape, "A Light Meditation" came out of that setup as the quality and detail was not quite what we needed.

In 1991 we started to use some of my music/sound for the (3 to 4 minute harmonic (going to black) or for the 10 to 20 minute Zygon (type) low frequency sound sequences of the theater experience.

Shortly before Mel passed Dorothy showed interest in the (new music possibilities). We worked together on a somewhat limited basis until Mel passed. After that music became part of our lives. We invested in a fairly extensive music and recording studio. We had musicians, throat singers, poets, and vocalists who came though the theater recording with us. It was a very spacey time.

When Mel passed I had never taken part in producing the live theater experience. After a few months we did an hour or 2 of dry runs and it seemed possible. For the next five and one-half years, Dorothy and I did the live theater performance. The one aspect of it we didn't do was the live painting sequence that Mel used to create on the overhead projectors. Starting with a tray of dye masked by a dark gel in front of the overhead projector he would "reveal" a live painting over the course of a musical cut.

In 1994 we started to rent professional SVHS cameras and created live video again specifically for our music. We setup our projection booth to focus on a screen hanging 15 feet into the theater and started to get the quality of images we needed.

In early 1995 a producer (Neil London) approached us with the idea of taking the Lumonics art form and video national thru a video presentation. We hired Neil and his friend (Bernard Hirshenson) a nationally known videographer - to shoot and produce the footage with the latest Beta SP equipment over a 10-day shoot. We got a lot of great footage, spending a much of our capital only to find that shooting and editing was only 5 -10% of the cost of getting something out into the world (the marketing and promotion). We cut off doing anything more with Neil shortly thereafter.

Going into the studio with Neil had taught us how to prepare for and deal in an editing suite at $150-250 an hour, so we did create our own tapes from BetaSP footage and our previous footage over the next few years. We sold maybe a thousand videotapes in the next 6 years period, but nowhere near to covering what we had spent.

The idea of at least partially automating the theater experience had been around since 1990, when I had set up a computer interface for our lighting control panel and bought a control board for the computer. It was not pursued any further at that time.

In 1999 my father passed leaving me a small inheritance. We put it all into a fast computer, DV capture card, software, and a video projector. We started converting all our old U-Mastic footage into DV. The idea of at least partially "automating" the theater experience came back up. Creating a tape from live performance video and then digitally editing and arranging it seemed a valid and interesting idea. At this time the Saturday shows were only happening once a month or every other week, and we were not doing much in the way of promotion.

In March 2000 an investor contacted us thru a man who had been to the theater for years. This investor was plugged into the stock market/investor capitol bubble at the time (we didn't realize how much) and proposed 4 Lumonics spaces "nightclubs" actually in London, Rome, New York, and Los Angeles. We started to work out the details of duplicating the experience and all that it would require. By late July 2000 the stock market capitol he was plugged into had evaporated and we were left with nothing to show after 4 months of planning.

After a month or so we decided that the experience we had gained in planning the "nightclub" venture was enough for us to do it on our own in the 2 warehouse bays that we had. It took about 2 months to set it up and with the DJs as promoters and the Internet exploding at the time we had a way to efficiently promote and create something lively. Having all these young people in such an environment was a blast for both them and us. It was amazing to see so many of them truly appreciated being given a space like Lumonics to experience in. We kept the music from totally taking over as it does in most club type situations. The theater was always a quieter alternative to the Nitelite dance space. There was a safety and beauty to it that the young were not used to. At the end of each night for 30-40 minutes we would do a video combined with live projection for these audiences. The reception was amazing. We even played some classical once in a while. One time one of the "raver girls" got up at the end and did an accapella classical song. The communication and mutual respect that we had with these young people was an emotional bridge that most people don't have in their lives.

The video was really taking off in this period. I would create relatively finished video clips of 5 - 40 seconds in length; Dorothy would choose the music and do a basic arrangement of the clips and timing. I would do the final tweaking relative to time, color, musical changes, and overall quality. Some of the video started to be created from digital sources. Magazine photos, movies, photos and video of industrial objects were taken into the digital realm where they became unrecognizable relative to their original form. It certainly looked like a "music video" although that was not our goal or intention. We were just doing what pleased us with the forms that we had created.

In 2002, just when we had just started to make some money with the theater/dance party the Rave Task Force raided almost all the venues in South Florida that were doing dance parties. We had some building code violations (work done without permits) and we have basically been closed since except for an 8-month grace period in late 2003 to June 2004.

In late 2003 I got interested in the possibilities of LEDs. I though of the dance floors we had done in the past and looked to apply LEDs to the idea. It turns out that every large lighting company was developing some kind of LED lighting at the same time and they just weren't out on the market yet. We had already invested a bit of money into it and had to pull back.

The upside of the LED experience is that they are a quite different type of light source than we had been dealing with previously. Dorothy has created 4 new works using LEDs as a light source. The method we use is not to see the LEDs but use them for backlighting. One of the works (backlighting a painting) in a black light box actually creates a dimension thru the color placement where one part of the painting jumps toward you a few inches. I think the LED lighting will produce a growing new avenue of works.

BARRY RAPHAEL

I met the Tanners at the perfect time in my life. It was the fall of 1971 . . . I was 24 years old. Teaching junior high school in Chicago had its problems. I was looking for a breakthrough, both in my vocation and my personal life. Can you live a counter-cultural meaningful existence in the heart of the city?

I had already dropped out once to travel around the country and lived communally for five months in southern Oregon. While it was a great learning experience, especially for a "city-fied" person, I didn't see a meaningful future there. I somewhat reluctantly returned to give teaching another try, bringing knowledge I had gained from an alternative lifestyle, including a greater sense of spirituality, to the classroom and to my life. I taught school during the day, and took graduate education courses at night and on the weekend, majoring in guidance and counseling. I thought of going into "radical counseling," a new career option I read about in the *Whole Earth Catalog*, i.e. counseling students in alternative and meaningful ways of working inside and outside of the established system. I was a hippie and embraced the counter-culture. I was afraid of "selling out" and being co-opted by the establishment. When years later, I heard the Neil Young song with the refrain, "Better to burn out than to fade away," it reminded me of how I lived back then. I had my left foot in the world and my right

Barry Raphael buffing dowles, 1976.

foot out, and felt an inward pull on my right side, which I resisted as much as I could. Though I was surrounded by friends, many of whom I knew since childhood, I also felt alone...on a journey that few of them shared.

THE BRIDGE TO LUMONICS

My breakthrough was soon to come, although not how I would have expected it: through my mother, who would have been the last person to encourage my counter-cultural journey. She was a card-carrying member of the establishment, and longed for me to get my "card." She was a successful travel agent in Chicago who was handling travel arrangements for Jerry Spiegel, the son of her long-time friend. Jerry would often fly to Miami to teach classes at Miami-Dade Community College. My mother had a lot of respect for him and thought he would give me proper career direction. She did not know that Jerry, after working for Mayor Richard J. Daley for many years, was beginning to embark on a new life's journey that coincided with mine. We could both learn from each other. I called him a few times, and he was difficult to meet because of his schedule . . . . We had a nice rapport on the phone, and he aroused my curiosity.

Jerry had a background in psychology and counseling. He was involved with encounter group workshops in the Psychology Department at Miami-Dade at a time when universities were bringing in the concept of "classes without walls," and breaking out of the traditional schoolroom structure.

Jerry told me that a few of the instructors brought him to a magical Theatre in Miami called Lumonics, and he got very excited about the concept. He encouraged Mel and Dorothy Tanner to move Lumonics to Chicago, and arranged for them to visit. By this time, I had met with Jerry a few times, and I was stoked about his description of the Theatre and the Tanners.

When Mel and Dorothy arrived in Chicago, I instantly bonded with them. It seemed my life could change in a way that I desperately longed for. The next step was to see the Theatre in Miami, and my upcoming Christmas vacation was a perfect time.

And then it happened. I walked into the Theatre and the vibration affected me profoundly. I never encountered a space filled with such spirituality, creativity and imagination. It was like a higher-consciousness UFO landed on Earth. Lumonics was a higher calling for me, and something I wanted to be part of for the rest of my life.

The day I returned to Chicago after the holiday, I resigned my job to devote all my time to finding the right location for the Theatre. I felt I was on a mission that couldn't wait. I was confident I would see my students eventually at Lumonics for field trips, where the power of the non-verbal experience could accelerate learning in a way that I couldn't accomplish in the classroom. Lumonics was the ultimate field trip.

Jerry Spiegel and I searched for the right location, but nothing felt right. My savings were being depleted. The Tanners suggested that I consider moving to Miami temporarily, offering me employment in a retail furniture store project they were involved with, while Jerry continued to search unsuccessfully for a place in Chicago.

By March 1972, Miami was my new home . . . Lumonics was my new life. I have been part of the project ever since. I look back at that time and see how I acted on trust and instinct. I followed the "wisdom of insecurity" into a new world.

NO OPERATING MANUAL

It has always been up to everyone to do what is possible for the betterment of Lumonics, which in turn would benefit each person's development. It brings to mind the quote of James Barrie, author of Peter Pan: "Those who bring sunshine into the lives of others cannot keep it from themselves."

Mel and Dorothy created an atmosphere for "greater good" to happen. While Mel had the air of a person who was all-knowing, he was humble and also not afraid to show his vulnerabilities. I remember in the early days, Mel telling us how essential it is for each of us to take responsibility. Neither Mel nor Dorothy liked the position of telling us what to do or giving us all the answers. They raised questions and encouraged us to think for ourselves. Dorothy expressed a confidence and self-assuredness without conceit, the wisdom "of an old soul." Their combination of introversion and extroversion created a dynamic force…they were "plugged" into each other on levels that I had never seen before in a relationship; they could easily finish each other's sentences. They both felt a responsibility for our well-being.

When Mel passed away in 1993, Dorothy took on an enormous responsibility to lead the way. She brought all of us out in ways that were more dormant while Mel was alive. It was a time to wake up, which is also the name of a song Dorothy composed, and a time of great change and creativity.

Dorothy decided to convert Mel's studio space into a Gallery for people to enjoy after the performances. She also began to collaborate very closely with Marc in composing music and video art. She also wrote lyrics that became known as "Cosmic Rap." Dorothy has been a remarkable demonstration for all of us.

While Dorothy and Mel always consulted with each other on their art, Mel generally lighted his pieces internally and Dorothy lighted hers externally. Now Dorothy has been focusing on internally lighted wall pieces that have a relationship to Mel's work yet have their own originality. The use of LED lighting gives her work a new quality.

The Tanners always showed their respect and appreciation for our dedication and our willingness to live outside of the "cookie cutter mold." What is in front of us to

do always determines the action. We write the manual as
we go.

BARBARA UNGAR

On the Friday evening of December 7, 1972 my friend Mark took me to Lumonics. The most awesome place I have ever experienced. Another world was the feeling with the most peaceful vibe, beautiful lights. The Art/wall pieces seemed to blend into each other.

I was introduced to Mel & Dorothy Tanner, Jocelyn Tanner, Louise Dillon, Barry Raphael & some friends, but I never spoke a word after hello.

When Mel & Dorothy heard about my ulcer they put me on a brown rice diet for a month, but I continued for another month. I had not felt that good in years.

Mel Tanner was a unique entity. I felt he was different when looking into his eyes experiencing the calm, peaceful vibration that radiated within him. Dorothy & I bonded like two people that have been friends for many lives. The psychic side of my life began to emerge. We knew what each other would say and think often. Mental pictures of events that were to happen became more frequent.

During the first several years I was learning how to trust myself and have faith that we would be provided for. Believing that you can & do create your own reality was as important as making a living. Life was very enriching & I could "cure" myself.

The days were filled with sewing and designing clothing with Dorothy and whatever work needed to be done.

I worked with Mark, Mel & Dorothy making their art and contacting people regarding the Theatre. Through the years I have taken care of the office work, organizing kids shows, built up everyone's credit, and other responsibilities regarding running Lumonics and also our personal life. I am grateful for my many experiences thru the years.

RITCH MOSIAS

I found Lumonics through a drummer named "Hodeen" who I had assisted in some drum circles. As a result, I was invited to Lumonics in June 1995. The event featured a very special light and sound show by Dorothy Tanner and Marc Billard, followed by a drum circle.

When I walked into the main theatre area, I was enveloped by a myriad of beautiful multi-colored art, lighted both internally and externally, not only floor sculptures but also wall- mounted.

The sounds were a wonderful blend of new age and world percussion/world beat in its entire sonic splendor. I felt energized yet lightened as if all my troubles and woes were lifted from my shoulders. It was a beautiful experience. The drumming was a relaxing way to consummate a memorable evening.

In retrospect, I realize that event was a spiritual epiphany offering an alternative to my past and present life's path. During a ten-year period, I have been with five very special people who invited me into their lives to share Lumonics. I developed a special friendship and bond with one of the group members, Barbara. She exemplifies qualities that I admire and look for in a mentor and role model.

Through the years, I have had many memorable and positive experiences with student groups that came to Lumonics for the light and sound performance followed by a drumming workshop. One in particular involved leading a group of autistic children and others who were developmentally challenged. The amazing interaction and their musical responses revealed an outpouring of genuine love. Not only did the children participate but all of the staff. "It was awesome," was the reaction.

Lumonics is presently going through another transitional phrase in its metamorphic evolution. I am looking forward to new possibilities that will further my development spiritually, mentally, and emotionally, and will positively affect others.

LUMONICS CONCERTS

UNTITLED CONCERTS: 1972-1974

Barry Raphael

We began to title the events in 1972 (we referred to the Lumonics events as concerts) that came at a time when we were all together for about a year and a half.

Barry Raphael arrived in March of 1972, Marc Billard and Barbara in Dec. of 1972. Other crewmembers besides Mel and Dorothy were Jocelyn Tanner (Mel's sister) and Louise Dillon, a long-time associate who met the Tanners in Syracuse, NY.

We had just completed a lighted dance floor, ceiling, and sound system for a new nightclub in Lexington, KY, The Library, co-owned by business mogul, John Brown. It provided some important income at the time.

When we ordered the sound components for The Library, we ordered additional components for the Theatre such as new speakers and two Phase Linear amps, one of which we use to this day.

That greatly improved the Theatre sound system; we added a Metrologic helion-neon laser which I found in a *Herbach and Rademan Catalog* in the elementary school library where I was substitute teaching; and new light sculptures, with Marc being the main shop person.

We also built additional seating, with Barbara using her knowledge of sewing and Dorothy and Mel designing the furniture. We would go to the "Fabric District," not too far from our location in the Design District, and buy "fun fur" (synthetic plush fabric in solid and also striped patterns). Eventually these "envelopes" of shredded foam covered with these luxurious fabrics replaced the waterbeds which would occasionally leak and inflatable furniture which would also leak air.

Other changes in the Theatre: we used a reflective paint for the front projection wall so that it was more reflective, and used paneling to curve the front walls.

The Herald had listings of events ("Best Bets") in the Friday edition. The deadline for submission was Tuesday. Every Tuesday morning, I would go to Lumonics and get the title of the concert from Mel and Dorothy who always came up with gems. I would quickly type it, and drive down to *The Miami Herald*, about 10-15 minutes away from 59th Terrace, and give it to the editor. It helped bring us many people and was practically the only way we got people, except for a call list that we established to notify people who attended previous events. Newspaper articles were a big help in expanding our audience; newspaper advertising was very occasional.

The listings with the titles went from March of 1974 to April of 1975. The editor of the section changed, and we lost our regular listing. It also came at a time where *Laserium* came into the area and took over a Wometco-owned Theatre on Lincoln Road, and did extensive advertising. *Laserium* got a regular listing instead of us. (Wometco was the company of the Wolfson family that had extensive media holdings in South Florida including WTVJ-TV.)

I was struck with the reality that someone new could come into the area and do such extensive advertising and promotion and could be a "household name" within a matter of days, and *Lumonics* would remain more unknown. I don't think *Laserium* lasted a year in South Florida although installations in planetariums around the U.S. were quite successful. In one sense, *Laserium* helped our business because it provided a reference point. People would call on the phone and ask how it was different from *Laserium*, or after the evening, would say how much more they enjoyed *Lumonics*.

CONCERT TITLES:
1974-1975

03/30/74 "Rites of Spring"
04/06/74 "In Search of the Miraculous"
04/13/74 "Midnight Easter Concert
04/20/74 "Journey into a Warehouse"
04/27/74 "The Venusian Way"
05/04/74 "Atlantean Sojourn"
05/11/74 "Space Signals"
05/18/74 "Golden Age"
05/24/74 "Mercurial Wonderland"
06/01/74 "Variations on a Violet Vibration"
06/08/74 "Inside a Split Second"
06/15/74 "A Light Ceremony"
06/22/74 "The Light Sound of the Moon"
06/29/74 "Wind Sounds and Light Colors"
07/06/74 "Spacial Planes and Outer Things"
07/13/74 "Light Shimmers on a Sound Wave"
07/20/74 "A Light Journey with Sound Company"
08/03/74 "The Sound of Light"
08/10/74 "Light Waves and Solar Sounds"
08/17/74 "Color, Sounds in a Light Field"
08/31/74 "In the Light of a Sound Chamber"

09/07/74 "Inside Outer Space"
09/14/74 "Stellar Sounds with a Light Chorus"
09/21/74 "Color Shadows in Light Sound"
09/28/74 "Light Prisms Thru Sound Bars"
10/05/74 "Light Scales the Sound Harmonies"
10/12/74 "In Light We Trust, In Sound We Color"
10/19/74 "the Light Dance of the Sound Fantastic"
10/26/74 "Sound Peaks in Light Valleys"
11/02/74 "Light Waves on a Sound Sea"
11/09/74 "A Light Bath with Sound Effects"
11/16/74 "A Light Source with Heavy Sound"
11/23/74 "The High Charge of Light and Sound"
11/30/74 "Sound and Light Massage"
12/07/74 "The Clear Light of a Transparent Sound"
12/14/74 "A Light Manipulation with Sound Objectives"
12/21/74 "Meteor Showers and Light and Sound Flowers"
12/28/74 "A Light Journey to a Sound Place"
01/04/75 "A Light Play with a Sound Cast"
01/11/75 "A Light Thought with a Sound Report"
01/18/75 "A Light Balance on a Sound High"
01/25/75 "A Light Stroke with Sound Recognition"
02/01/75 "A Light Touch on a Sound Idea"
02/08/75 "The Speed of Light Reflected in a Sound Space"
02/15/75 "A Light Measurement on a Sound Rule"
02/22/75 "On the Light Side of a Sound Meeting"
03/01/75 "Soon the Light—And the Sound Thereafter"
03/08/75 "Sound Changes into Light Places"
03/15/75 "Light Speeds to Distant Sound
03/22/75 "A Light Extension Thru a Sound Connection"
03/29/75 "Now Hear the Sound and See the Light"
04/05/75 "A Future Light in a Present Sound"
04/12/75 "The Rites of Light in a Sound Season"
04/19/75 "A Right Light for a Left Sound"

INTRODUCTORY REMARKS
TO PERFORMANCES, 1990, 2000

FOR GOING TO BLACK
WITH "ZYGON TYPE SOUND AT END," 1990

(Mel)

Good Evening. Welcome to *Lumonics*. *Lumonics* is a specialized sensory environment. It utilizes light, sound, color, aroma and imagery. Its purpose is to relax and energize, to promote a sense of well being.

(Dorothy)

The last segment of each performance consists, not of music, but of sound, meditative sound and visuals designed to induce a deeper contemplative state. The relaxation and stimulation induced by these means can last for many hours and sometimes days.

(Mel)

The effects can be far-reaching. Thank you.

FOR GOING TO BLACK, 2000

(Marc)

Welcome to the *Lumonics* Light and Sound Theater. The performance you are about to experience will engage your feelings, your sense of sight, and your sense of hearing. Our goal is relax and energize, and stimulate your creativity and imagination. The tools we use are the light sculptures, music, lasers and projection techniques developed over the years at *Lumonics*. You are on the threshold of a very special performance that will take you on an unforgettable journey. In your mind you will see extraordinary abstract images that are your own creation. I suggest that you relax, clear your mind of any thoughts, take a deep breath and hold it for a few seconds, then let the air out slowly. Forget about your neighbor and become totally aware of the space you are in.

For the full impact of the experience, remain as quiet as you can, and remember that through *Lumonics* you can see the mind at its best. In this environment you are safe and free. Let the performance begin.

AT THE END, 2000

(Dorothy)

Thank you for joining us tonight and allowing us the pleasure of sharing a *Lumonics* performance with you. My name is Dorothy Tanner and I regard this *Lumonics* space as my home, and I invite you to treat it as though it were yours. We'll be opening the portal to Nightlight Gallery shortly. Dance if you wish, lounge if you so desire. Extend and expand your experience here with us. Please feel free to remain in your seats as long as you like. Enjoy.

CONCERT FLYERS

COCONUT GROVE, FL
PROMOTIONAL FLYERS

Original Lumonics Flyer, 1970

PRESS RELEASE - FOR IMMEDIATE RELEASE

Mel and Dorothy Tanner are beginning the second year of LUMONICS
CONCERTS Saturday night September 25. Concerts will be given every
Saturday at 9:30 P.M.

The Lumonics experience has expanded and developed in power. The
performers continue to play with the viewer's sense of reality. New
light sculptures* have increased the dream quality of the environment.

The Tanners are artists (painter and sculptor) who have exhibited
work in galleries and museums in New York City. Their new medium
"Lumonics" employs music, electronics, painting and sculpture as a
simultaneous experience in a controlled space.

Concerts are never repeated or programmed. They are spontaneous
occurences. Artist and audience are involved in the experience as it
is happening.

Audiences who find this "far out" warehouse vary in size, shape,
style and age. Many return as friends with friends. They become
the kinetic element in an "unreal" space designed to contain them.
Here they take a trip into the "mind's eye" together and separately -
into another world or age . . . the "Age of Aquarius" perhaps.

*An invitation is extended to visit the Studio Gallery Tuesday thru
Saturday between 1:00 and 6:00 P.M. or by appointment. Prices upon
request - commissions accepted.

LUMONICS   September 1971
355 N.E. 59 Terrace
Miami, Florida
759-1312   Concerts $4.00

LUMONICS

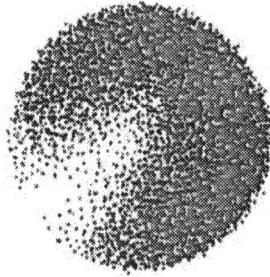

light and sound theatre

"every now and again, you come across something
new and exciting in the world of design that is
difficult to describe, one of the most unusual yet
beautiful experiences in the world of art."

miami herald

"lumonics--an enveloping experience in sight and
sound."

miami news

concert every sat. 9:45 pm - adm. $6.00 reserv. only
LUMONICS 355 n.e.59 ter., miami, fla. phone - 759 - 1312

Flyer from 1974

LUMONICS
light and sound encounter
"An experience of brave new world dimensions."
— Miami Magazine
"One of the most unusual yet beautiful experiences in the world of art."
Miami Herald
"An enveloping experience in sight and sound."
Miami News
Wed. Fri. Sat. From 9:00 P.M.-1:00 A.M.
Adm. $6.00 Reservations Phone 759-1312
Lumonics 355 N.E. 59 Ter. Miami

Flyer, 1978

An Experience Like No Other . . .

LUMONICS

LUMONICS
25 Broad Street
Bangor, Maine
04401
942-2202

A Gallery of Design, Light and Sound
Blended With Technology To Create
A Performance For Your Mind.

UNIQUE ENVIRONMENT

A unique environment has come to Bangor. . .the Lumonics Performing Gallery. Created by Mel Tanner and associates, Lumonics utilizes luminal sculpture, laser, sound and video to create an art experience like none other you have ever seen. Imagine — an "art gallery" which comes alive — with sound, motion and lights. . . that's Lumonics.

STIMULATION/RELAXATION

An experience that stimulates and relaxes. . . that's Lumonics. How? Well, the Lumonics performance "speaks" with your subconscious, by communicating with the non-verbal part of your brain — the right hemisphere. Scientific studies show this section of the brain is the one which deals with visual imagery, fantasy, emotions — the ingredients which generate creativity. The Lumonics Experience soothes your body with a bath of sound and light, leaving the right hemisphere of your mind free to explore. A stimulating relaxation.

AND, IT'S A WHOLE LOT OF FUN!

Science aside, Lumonics is just plain fun. Imagine being seven years old and finding a room full of wonderful new toys and images. That's one impression you get from the Lumonics Gallery. Enter a room full of delightful luminal sculpture that's yours to explore. Hidden amidst the art, you'll find gently trickling fountains.

Wait. . .there's more. Sink into one of the many plump pillows or couches, take off your shoes. "The curtain of light is rising" and the gallery is ready to perform. As the lights dim, you are immersed in a wave of synthesized sound. The sculpture glows and throbs to the tempo. The atmosphere of the gallery comes alive with laser projection and video art. You are surrounded by a total art experience. Lumonics is a concert for your mind.

Once more the tempo changes and the performance slows dow . You are again bathed in the soothing sound of the fountains and the glowing lights of the sculpture.

You owe it to yourself to experience Lumonics. . .a unique entertainment that stimulates as it relaxes. But we warn you — it is extremely habit forming!

Lumonics comes to Bangor after eleven years of successful performances in Miami, Florida and San Diego, California. Since Lumonics opened to the public, it has provided special performances for many groups including schools and universities, the gifted and disturbed, drug rehab programs and art and music organizations.

You're able to experience the Lumonics Performing Gallery in Bangor, Maine because Mel Tanner and his associates find the area a comfortable place to work and develop ideas that they plan to eventually promote in other areas

The Lumonics Performing Gallery is available as a unique setting for club meetings and private functions by simply reserving your special time.

Each performance is unlike any other. You'll want to attend often, after your initial visit.

LUMONICS . . .
An Experience
in Revitalizing
Your Mind

117

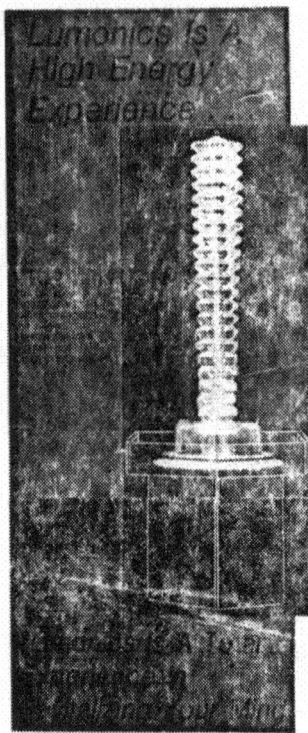

October 14, 1988

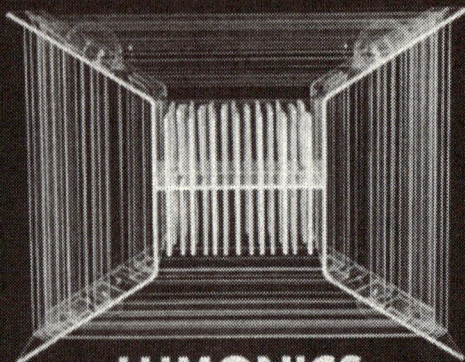

Flyer, 1998

Flyer, 1989

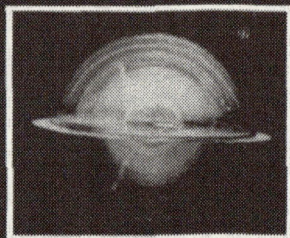

Flyer (back), 1989

Poster, 1989

Flyer, 1994

DRUM DANCE THEATRE Presents:

LUMONICS CONVERGENCE

All are welcome.
Witness a moving ceremony.
Live drumming,
copal, and meditative vision.

3017 NW 50th Street
Fort Lauderdale

South of Cypress Ck. Rd. (McNab, or 62nd) off NW 31st Ave. (Lyons)

Mayan Connection
with **to the Starz**

Howard and
Dean   Jim Reed
Master Drummer/Percussionist   *Meditation Facilatator*

Dr. Barry · Tim O'Donnell
Healing Facilatator   *Master Musician/Craftsman*

Friday, May 12th · 8:30 PM
Drum Dance Theatre *inside* Lumonics • (305) 979-3161 • Only $10

Poster, 1994

LUMONICS

AN ASTONISHING
21st CENTURY ADVENTURE

CREATED AND
PERFORMED

BY

DOROTHY
TANNER
&
MARC
BILLARD

SATURDAY
EVES.

8:30 PM

ADM. $20

FOR INFO
954-979-3161

LUMONICS - THE PERFORMANCE

an EXPLOSIVE mixture of ELECTRONIC LIGHT
SCULPTURES, PROJECTION, LASERS, HIGH ENERGY MUSIC
that DELIGHTS the EYE and EAR, FIRES the
IMAGINATION, and EXPANDS the MIND.

FEATURING COSMIC RAP

SATURDAYS 8:30 PM   RESV. REQUIRED   ADM. $20
AFTER THE PERFORMANCE:
JOIN IN INTERACTIVE DRUMMING - INSTRUMENTS PROVIDED

A FANTASTIC VISUAL UNIVERSE

LUMONICS   3017 NW 60 ST.   FT. LAUDERDALE   954-979-3161
VISIT OUR WEB SITE AT   http://www.lumonicslightandsound.com

Flyer, 1996

a night with

**harmonic
motion**

Saturday 22 November 1997

at

Lumonics

3017 NW 60 St.
Ft. Lauderdale, FL
(954)979-3161

9:00 PM - Gallery doors open at 8:30
$25 - reservations suggested

DOROTHY TANNER and MARC BILLARD of Lumonics commence the
evening with a battery of projectors, 50 electronic light sculptures, and
lasers which will soar to the Progressive Middle Eastern music and dance
of Harmonic Motion.

with :

JOE ZEYTOONIAN - oud, voice, and percussion
MYRIAM ELI - dance and percussion

Following the performance join the percussion ensemble and dance circle.
Bring your drums and shakers, or Lumonics will provide instruments for
your use.

http://www.lumonicslightandsound.com

Flyer, 1997

DJED Celebration
Celebrate the Fall Equinox
Saturday September 21 Doors open at 11 pm -$15
Live Drumming over Trance Music Midnite til Sunrise
After 1 am – Admission $20

Autumnal Equinox Drum Joy Ecstatic Dancing

Ecstatic Dancing Lumonics opens 10 pm–Multi-culture Dance

Lumonics is a specialized sensory environment of light and sound. The mood altering atmosphere that envelops you as soon as you step thru the door continues throughout the evening. Wander through the various gallery rooms comprised of magical light sculptures suspended from the walls or rising from the floor; each with its own cryptic message. The 35-foot front wall becomes the receiver for the multi-layered imagery that will keep you mesmerized. The performance is the synergy of the light sculptures, water fountains, a battery of projectors, video art, lasers, and the spontaneous creativity that transforms technology into living art.

The Ecstatic Dancing is not a performance, it is an experience. The purpose is for you to release stored emotions like anxiety or joy. In modern times there is no socially acceptable way to release negative emotions like worry, grief, fear, anger or sadness.

In order for emotions to be released they must be fully expressed. When the music folds into the meditation the rhythm picks you up and you start to move and sway. As the rhythm picks up speed you begin to dance faster and faster and faster until you are emotionally and physically spent and spiritually uplifted.

We Dance to release shame, blame and guilt and build conscious intention.
We Dance to release worry and connect to the intelligence of our ancestors.
We Dance to mend the broken heart and build unconditional Love.
We Dance to release anger and create forgiveness.
We Dance to release fear and build courage.

Dr. George Love Acupuncture Physician 888-766-8711 www.geoloveheals.com
www.lumonics.net for directions 954-979-3161

Flyer, 1998

Lumonics
presents
an evening with
Crazy fingers
Dec 20th

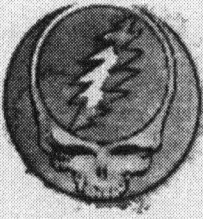

"Difficult to describe, beautiful and unusual, the Lumonics
Light and Sound Theatre is hard to compare or
judge, comprehend even, because it has no peers. It is different, something unto
itself, and not entirely of this world."
Ken Piutnicki, staff writer, The Miami Herald

Tanner Studio / Lumonics
3017 NW 60th Street
Fort Lauderdale, FL 33309
PH 954.979.3161 „FX 954.972.5802,
, 1.800.360.6811

"Lumonics brings together light sculptures,
water sculptures, performance art,
digital video, laser art, dance, and music,
all in one blow-your-mind complex."

www.crazyfingers.net

We cordially invite you into a state of comfort and awareness
LUMONICS
Light Museum and Gallery,
A Multi-Sensory Environment
Voted "Best Art Experience"
"Thrilling performance art that brings together light sculptures, water fountains, digital video lasers, and high energy sound, all in one blow-your-mind complex"
-New Times
"New and exciting...One of the most unusual yet beautiful experiences in the world of art"
-Miami Herald
"Like another world. Lumonics is better seen than described."
-Sun Sentinel
11.29.03
Space Signals:
A sound and light performance by D.Tanner, M. Billard
Special Guests:
Aurapool The Fusion Band
Inspired by Phish and Pink Floyd
Ellen Thea (Resident Poet)
12.6.03
Inside Outer Space: Light and sound experience, excerpts from Dark Side of the Moon
Special Guests:
Serpentine (Mystic Trance-Pop Singer) and
James Garcia (Percussionist) debuts Chakra Mysteries and Intimacies
Drum Circle Facilitated by Rich Mosies
3017 NW 60th St., Ft. Lauderdale 954-979-3161
[www.lumonics.net]
Open Saturdays at 8:30pm
Adm. $15 • Reservations Suggested

Flyer, 2003

MUSIC AND VIDEO TAPES

Spices of the World

Tanner/Billard

Spices of the World
#2

Tanner/Billard

VIDEO TITLES: 1979 TO 2004

Light Side of the Moon
(silent video) 1980
A visual interpretation of the classic Pink Floyd album, *Dark Side of the Moon.*

"The Choice is Yours"
(musicvideo) 1980
Ccreated as part of the CETA Grant in San Diego, CA, A semi-abstract presentation of the harm done to the environment and the awareness of how to make the world a better place.

A Light Meditation
(video) 1980
Iincludes abstract imagery and the light sculptures.

A Slow Boat to Ecstasy
(music video) 1994
Relaxation video.

Pleidian Chants
(music) 1994
"Well-conceived and expertly executed, the music ranks with the finest in the genre."(JAM Magazine)

Un-Limiting Yourself
(spoken word, musicvideo) 1994
Commissioned by Dr. Kathryn Mickle, the video combines Dr. Mickle's sensitive dialog and hypnotic suggestions with the colorful, imagery and meditative sound of Tanner/Billard.

A Spacious Moment in Time
(musicvideo) 1995

Inside a Split Second
(musicvideo) 1995

Color Vapors
(musicvideo) 1996

Cosmic Rap
 (music CD and video) 1997
Meditation in a Box. The music's varied textures draw from jazz, electronic, and classical. Dorothy's spoken word is expressed with humor, understanding, and finesse.

Spices of the World
(music CD) 1999
Adventures in music that cut across styles and ethnicities; blending Middle Eastern, African, Latin, and Ambient Electronica—a "cosmic stew"—transporting the listener into an etheric space.

Spices of the World 2
(music CD) 2000
Further adventures in world music

Space Visuals and Soundscapes, Vol. 1.
(musicvideo) 2003

The Art of Mel and Dorothy Tanner, Vol. 1.
(musicvideo) 2003

Pleidian Dawn
(musicvideo) 2003

Don't Let It Slip Away
(musicvideo) 2003

The Light Side of the Moon 1979

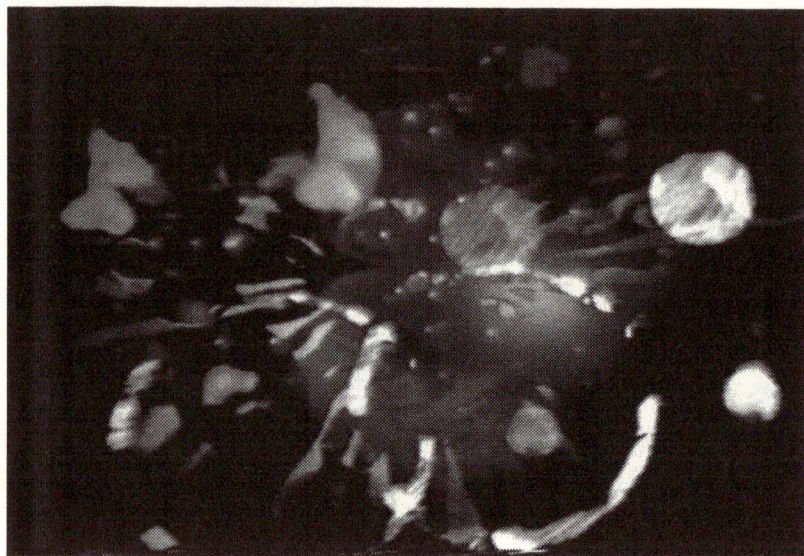

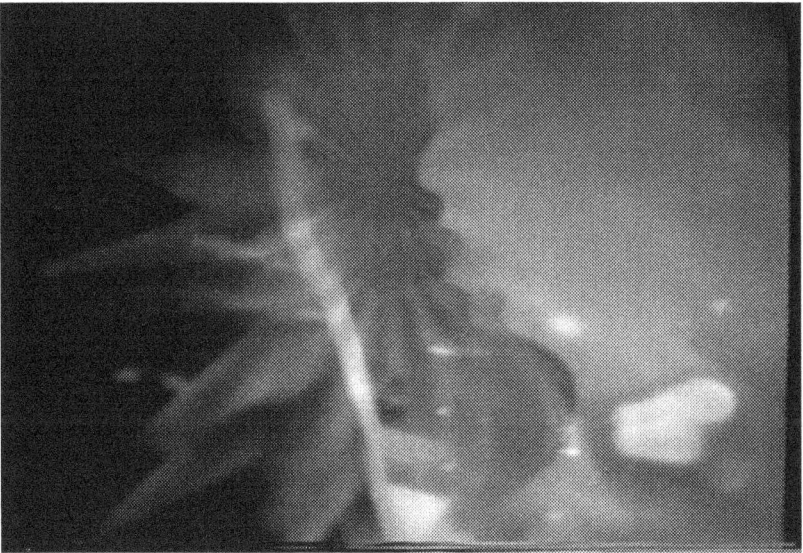

Ecology video 1980

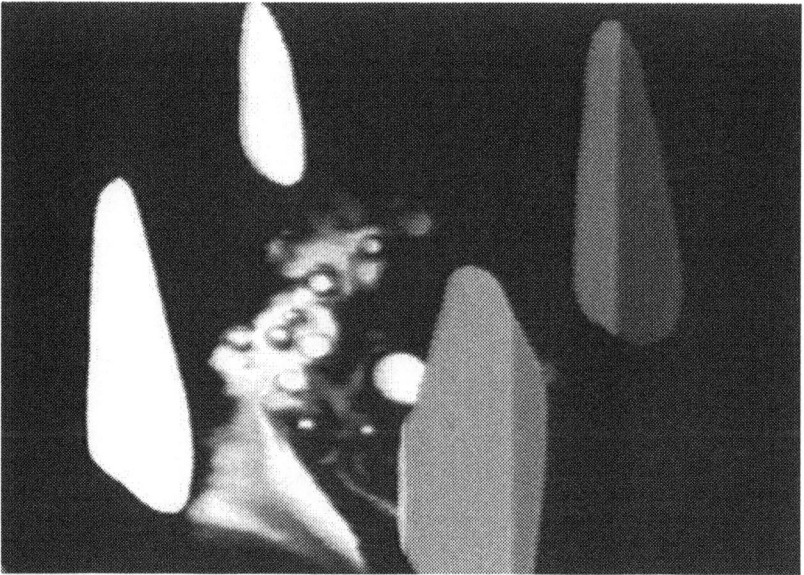

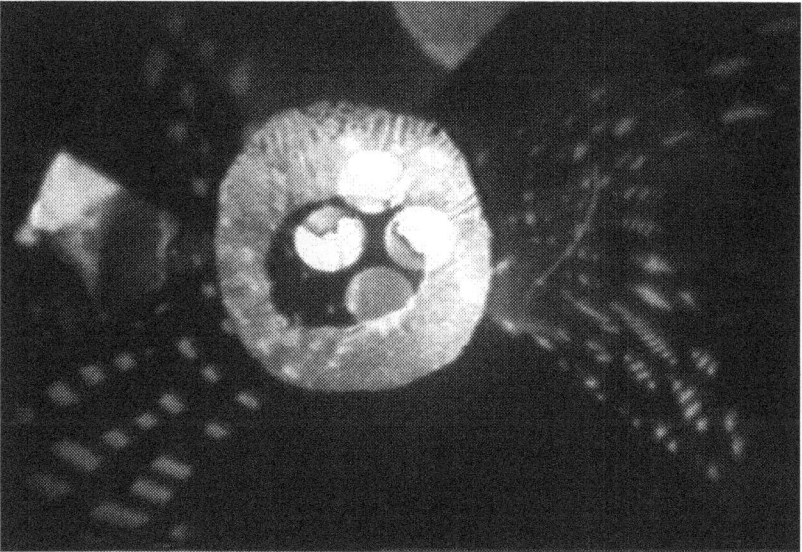

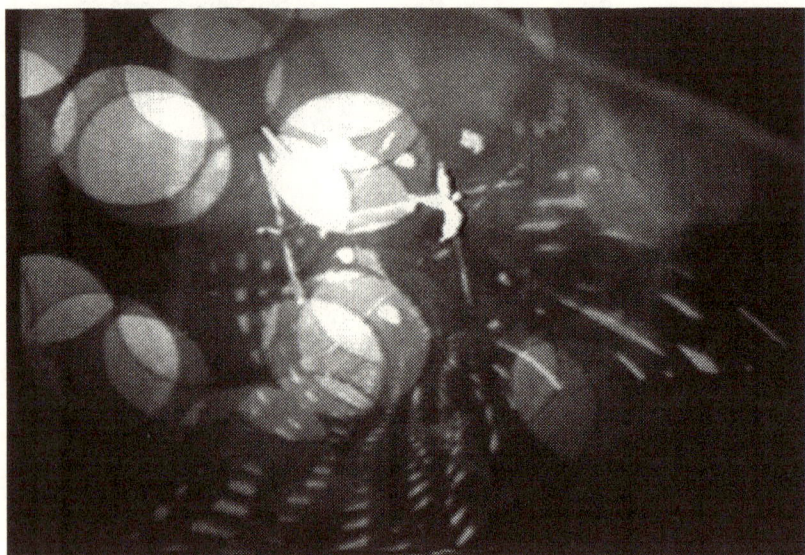

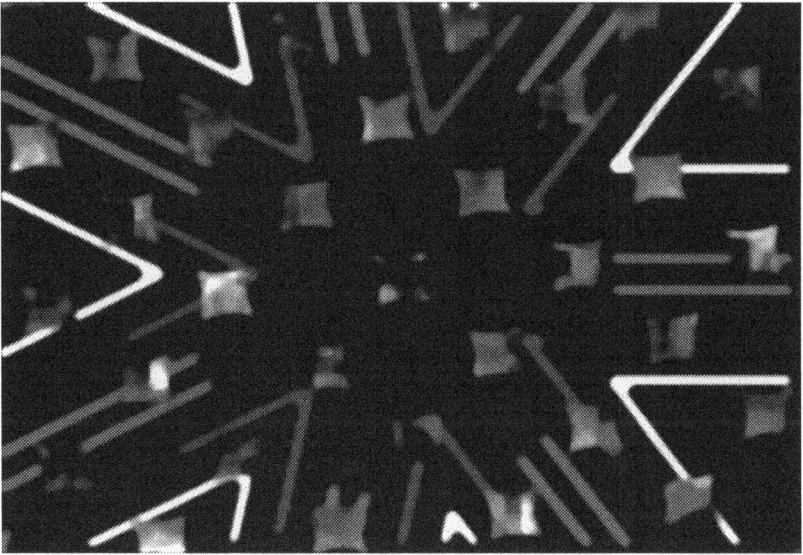

Arizona, 2004

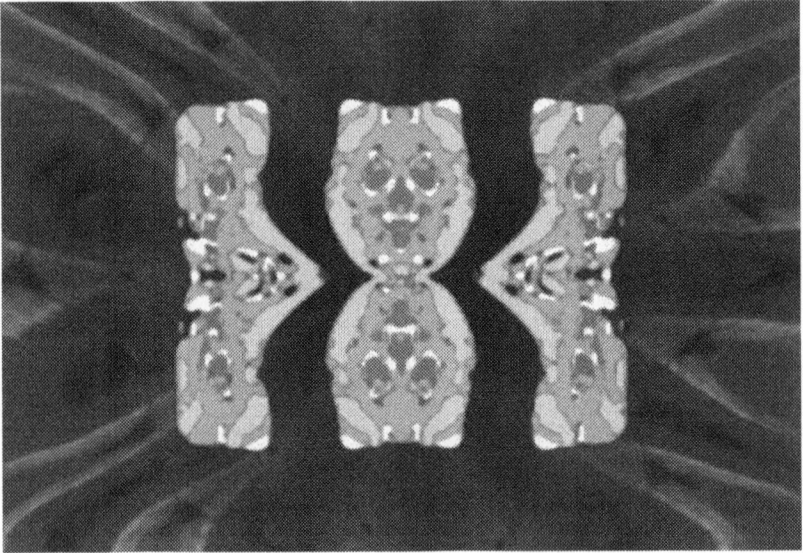

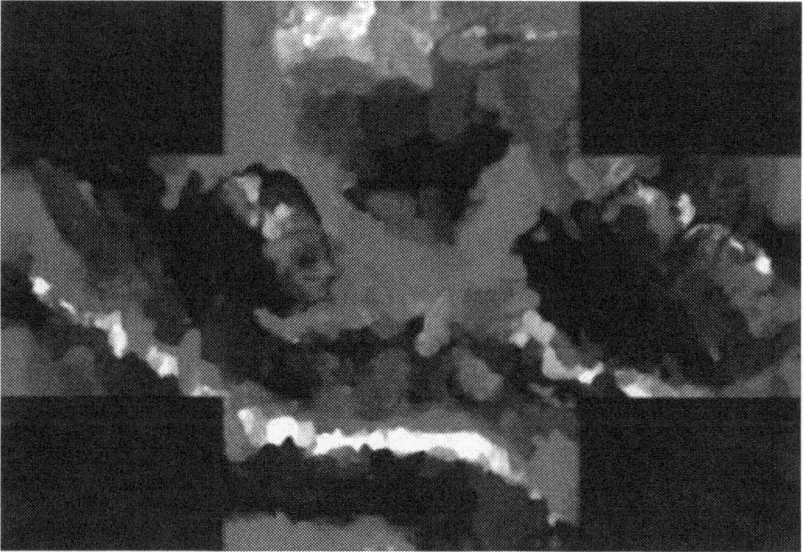

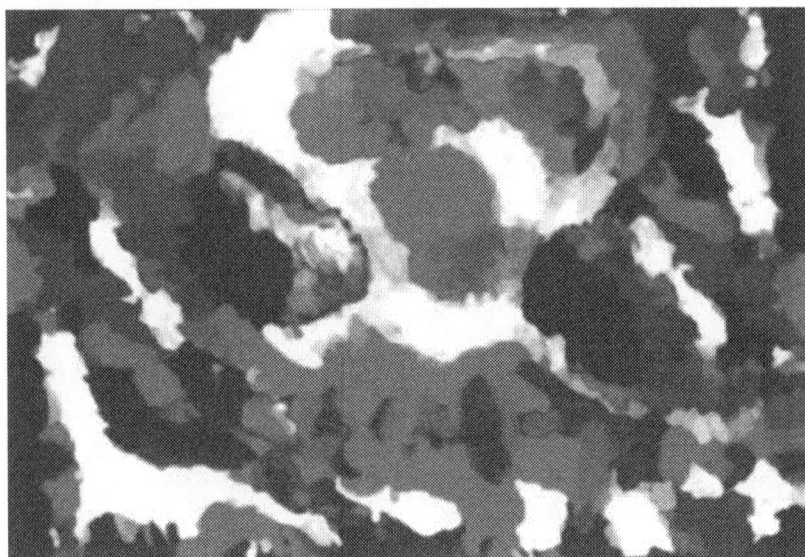

New Mexico, 2004

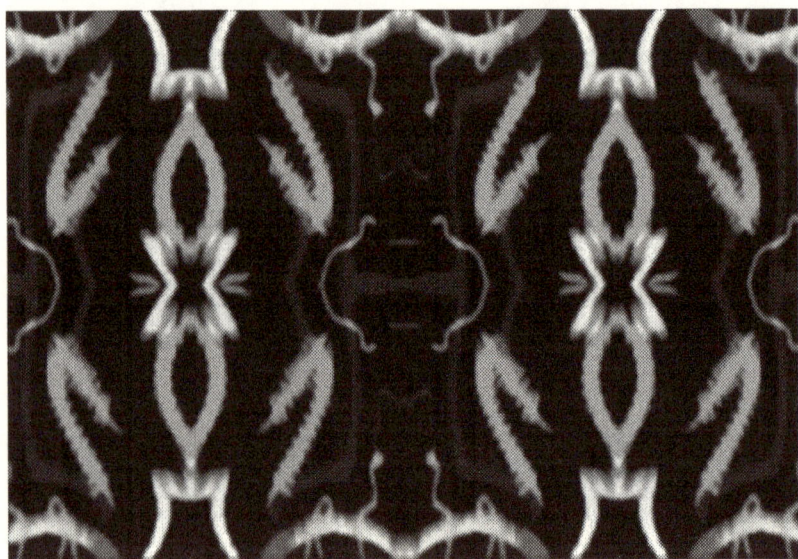

DON'T LET IT SLIP AWAY
VIDEO REVIEW

Peter Lavezzoli

Mel Tanner's light sculptures expanded the traditional concepts of both lighting and sculpture, while involving elements of each art form. His revolutionary acrylic
sculptures were viewed in the specific Lumonics setting.
Having experienced these light sculptures myself, it seems
clear to me that these creations were actually the seeds for
the audio/visual work that Dorothy Tanner and Marc
Billard have now produced. The medium of Mel Tanner's
geometric expressionistic light sculptures, has been refined
and expanded to Tanner/Billard's DVD productions, such
as *Pleiadian Dawn* and *Don't Let It Slip Away*, which can be
experienced in an environment of one's own choosing. The
experience produced by the Lumonics environment was
that of a sort of shrine. It is interesting that Mel and Dorothy
Tanner first created this environment in the 1960s while listening to and under the inspiration of psychedelic music.
The Tanner/Billard DVDs are an ideal marriage of light and
color patterns with repetitive electronic music, the
psychedelic music of today.

Electronica, the term that loosely describes several
types of electronically generated repetitive music, is the
logical progression of the amplified psychedelic music that

151

inspired the original *Lumonics* Theater environment. Tanner/Billard's electronic music uses elements of minimalism, where a fixed set of notes and rhythms are permutated in several interesting mathematical ways. This is a process that can be traced back to not only to twentieth century composers such as Terry Riley, but also to Indian classical music and other ancient traditions. In the Eastern and African cultures, music is a means to enlightenment, not an end in itself. Tanner/Billard's work invites the audience to be active participants rather than passive witnesses. This is part of an ancient science where musical and visual structures match specific states of consciousness.

One of the most important features of repetitive electronic music is that a set of frequencies and rhythms are repeated over and over, each frequency and rhythm coming back to the same place. This sets up a series of patterns in the nervous system of the listener, so that a specific psychological state is created. This teaches us something about universal structure. Sound is the highest medium through which we can experience the structure of the universe. If we believe that the universe is composed of vibrations, then we can understand how repetitive music, which the human nervous system can immediately assimilate, can lead to an understanding of universal structure.

"Meditainment" works within this understanding. Going back to the ancient practices of spiritual chant, from OM to Gregorian, music has always helped human beings explore their relationship to the universe.

We know that certain combinations of color have a profound effect on the emotions and the nervous system. When one steps into the Lumonics environment, one is immediately transported into states of both tranquility and creative stimulation. Tanner/Billard have brought this awareness of color and shape into DVD, allowing us to experience these sensations in our own environment, in our own time. The colors and shapes affect us at deeper levels of the mind. We feel like children again, free to explore and linger in this timeless realm of color and sound, with nothing demanding us to move on. In this space, we are free to let our minds wander in ways that we usually do not have time for. The imagination is reawakened in ways that bring us back to our earliest experiences of color and sound. What may have long seemed impossible in our minds becomes possible again. Ideas and visions that have been buried under the demands of everyday life are given the space to grow and flourish. We find ourselves becoming reacquainted with our dreams, and the courage to act upon them. Far from being solely geared towards inducing a state of calm and tranquility, these DVDs can motivate us to reawaken our own sense of artistic freedom that, for so many of us, is often dormant since childhood. The stimulating blend of color and sound encourages our minds to become more playful, more exploratory, giving us permission to create. Tanner/Billard have given us a wonderful tool for the mind, body, and spirit—a new opportunity for us to rediscover a sense of wonder.

THE MUSIC AND VISUALS OF TANNER/BILLARD

Barry Raphael

FROM A PRESS RELEASE

Dorothy Tanner and Marc Billard create the digital video art and world/electronica music that is an integral part of the Lumonics experience.

The music of Tanner/Billard is a highly original cross-cultural hybrid with influences of world music, electronic, techno, industrial, classical, and jazz. When the music is combined with their abstract multi-layered rich visualizations, using colors and forms I didn't even know existed, the effect is mesmerizing yet easy to "access" in the mind's eye, transporting you into a new universe of color and shape. How do you relax and energize at the same time? Start your DVD now...

Tanner and Billard have developed a style of music with an exotic feel; involving intriguing textures, percussive effects, world instruments and vocals. They are both deeply involved and excited by the potential that exists in today's technologically sophisticated music world. The

154

freshness, freedom, and richness that cross-cultural music sampling affords has inspired their recent work.

Dorothy and Marc began their musical collaboration in 1990. Marc had been experimenting with computers, synthesizers and midi since 1985. For Dorothy, music composition is as comfortable as creating sculpture, finding satisfying similarities between the two modalities.

The Tanner/Billard video art is a further development of the pioneering video art form of Dorothy and Mel Tanner (d.1993), beginning in 1978, and is rooted in the live visual performances that have taken place in the Lumonics Light and Sound Theatre, beginning in 1969.

BIBLIOGRAPHY

The Herald refers to *The Miami Herald*

Murphy, Kay, "Let There Be Light, *Tropic Magazine,The Herald,* May 26, 1968 (before Theatre, featured early lighted sculptures).

Von Maurer, Bill, "Décor You Can Get With,", *The Miami News,* May 23, 1969 (Hi-Fi Associates article, just prior to the Theatre).

Robbins, Dave, "A Completely New Art Form," *University of Miami Hurricane,* Sept. 18, 1970 (first review of Lumonics).

Tedeschi, David, "The Light Fantastic," *The Herald,* Nov. 13, 1970
"Tanner at Lumonics," *Free Press,* August 12, 1971.

Elliott, John, "Lumonics Theater Total Art Trip," *The Miami-Dade Downtowner,* Nov.5, 1973.

Marlowe, Jon, "It's 2,000 Light Years from Home," *The Miami News,* May 16, 1975.

Gubernick, Adrienne, "Art, Sound, Light Mix in Lumonics Concerts," *University of Miami Hurricane,* Oct. 26, 1976.

Bloomberg, Gigi, "Light Show Unearthly Trip," *Falcon Times*, Miami-Dade Community College, North Campus, Jan. 19, 1977.

Kesselman, Marc, "Lumonics Show Features Laser Symphonic Art," *University of Miami Hurricane*, April 1, 1977.

Klein, Marjorie, "Winkin', blinkin', and nod," *Miami Magazine*, March 1977.

Gillmon, Rita, "What is Lumonics," *The San Diego Union*, Sept.19, 1980.

Rice, Ed, "A Review of Lumonics: A 'Far Out' Place," *The Weekly Journal*, Nov. 4, 1981.

Furry, Eric, Lumonics: "Where Light, Music and Art Converge," *Sweet Potato*, Feb. 17, 1982.

Groswiler, Paul, "Let There Be Light: Sculpture Fuses Light and Sound," *Bangor Daily News*, March 20, 1982.

"Lumonics Wing Opens at Patricia Judith Gallery," *Boca Raton Life*, Nov. 1986.

Boccio, Rose, "'Mesmerizing' Art Form Lights Up Boca Gallery," *Sun-Sentinel*, Nov. 6, 1986.

Sheffied, Skip, Exhibit Glows in the Art at Boca Art Gallery," *Boca Raton Daily News*, Dec. 15, 1986.

Wolff, Millie, "Patricia Judith Gallery Features Contemporary Art at its Best," *Palm Beach Daily News*, Feb. 6, 1987.

Schwan, Gary, "Shining On," *The Palm Beach Post*, June 5, 1987.

Mann, Maybelle, "Lumonics Exhibit Opens in Boca: Dazzling, Dizzying Sculpture," *Jewish World*, Oct, 31, 1987.

"Lumonics," *Miami New Times*, May 4, 1988.

Heidelberg, Paul, "Art from the Beyond," *Sun-Sentinel*, June 19, 1988.

Shonkwiler, Bonnie, "The Dawning of a New Age, The Herald, June 26, 1988.

MacEnulty, Pat, "Lumonics Show Has an Otherworldly Atmosphere," *Sun-Sentinel*, 1989.

Plutnicki, Ken, "Light Show a Theater of the Mind," *The Herald*, 1989.

Lynn, Teri, "Lumonics: A New Way of Tripping," 25th *Parallel*, Sept. 1989.

Loret De Molac, Alex, "Lumonics: Tripping through time, space and light with the Tanners," New Miami Magazine, August, 1990.

Gallotta, Paul, "'Lumonics' Sound and Light Show a Natural High, *Eastsider*, Oct. 3, 1990.

Mills, Michael, "Tripping the Light Fantastic," *Palm Beach Post*, July 14, 1991.

Marx, Linda, "Taking a Trip on the Light Fantastic," *Palm Beach Life Magazine*, Dec. 1991.

Sims, Robert, "Gallery Claims More than Light Entertainment," *Eastsider*, April 22, 1992.

Silverstone, Marni, "Light Fantastic Trip," *Sun-Sentinel*, August 1, 1992.

Morgan, Roberta, "Play Tripper," *Miami New Times*, June 30, 1993.

Rose, Maxine, "Cosmo Theatre, *Around Town*, July 9, 1993.

Wilson, Gary, "Lumonics: The Light and Sound Fantastic," 1994.

Packwood, Amy, ""Lumonics: The Virtual Reality Music of the Future," *Spike*, Dec. 1994.

Segal, Jamie, "The Beat of a Different Drum, *The Chronicle*, Coral Springs High School, May 26, 1995.

Scott, Kristy, "Horizons Interview: Lumonics Light and Sound Theatre, *Horizons*, Sept. 1995.

Felberbaum, Mike, "Lumonics Offers Psychedelic Trip through Light and Time, The Chariot, Taravella High School, Dec. 1995.

Koretzky, Michael, "Tripping the Light Fantastic," *XS*, Feb, 14, 1995.

Koretzky, Michael, "The Scene: Bang the Drum Quickly at Lumonics," *Entertainment News & Views*, Aug. 4, 1995.

Shargel, Lee, "Lumonics Light and Sound Theatre: Entertainment for the 21st Century, *Center Stage*, Oct. 1995.

Morgan, Roberta, "Light and Sound from the 60's," *Daily Business Review*, Oct. 20, 1995.

Coate, Steve and Fritz, Tracy, "Lumonics: Escape to a World of Inspiration," The Observer, Broward Community College, Nov. 6, 1995.

Dillon, Louise, "New Light on Education," *United Dade Teachers Today*, March, 1996.

Mills, Michael, "Lumonics—Art as Environment," *Fountain*, May, 1996.

Warm, Dave, "...Tripping the Light Fantastic at Lumonics,", *XS Magazine*, July 9, 1996.

Koretzky, Mike, "Bright lights, big beats, and watery art, *XS Magazine*, June 24, 1997.

DellaRocca, Lenny, "The Cultural Café," *Coral Springs-Parkland Forum*, July 3, 1997.

Mills, Michael, "Ghosts in the Machines" *New Times,Broward-Palm Beach*, April 9, 1998.

Florin, Hector, "What a sight...to hear," *Sun-Sentinel*, August 2, 1999.

Crumpler, Ike, "Let there be Light," *Eastsider*, Nov. 24, 1999.

Ferri, John, "Lightheaded," New Times Broward-Palm Beach, Aug. 31, 2000.

Caplivski, David, "Lumonics Lights Up the Night, *The Knight*, Nova-Southeastern Univ., Jan. 24, 2001.

"Best Art Experience," *New Times Broward-Palm Beach*, April, 2001.

DJ Devon3, "Twenty-First Century Performance Art Specializing in Graphic Visualization and Mood-Altering Effects," (online) May 19, 2001.

Waas, Mitch, "MUSIC, LUMONICS, AND ME. A LIFE IN FLUX, CHAPTER ONE, 1968-2001, " (online), April 1, 2001.

"Best Dance Club," *New Times Broward-Palm Beach*, April, 2002.

DeMarzo, Wanda, "Rave Club Closed by New Drug Task Force," *The Herald*, May 31, 2002.

Soto, Alfred, "Past Present Future at the Lumonics Light Museum," *The Herald*, Aug. 9, 2002.

Budjinski, Jason, "Lumonics Wants to Light Up Your Life," *New Times Broward-Palm Beach*, Oct. 18, 2003.

Florin, Hector "Nourish Your Weary Soul at Lumonics," *The Herald*, Feb. 6, 2004.

Shear, Robin, "Hooked on Lumonics: Take a Walk on the Light Side in Fort Lauderdale, *Eastsider*, Jan. 22, 2004.

Hambright, Courtney, "Adrift in Translation," *New Times Broward-Palm Beach*, Feb. 26, 2004.

"Best Art Gallery," *New Times Broward-Palm Beach*, April, 2004.

EXHIBITION HISTORY

MEL TANNER

Solo Shows

1997   *Museum of New Arts*, Fort Lauderdale
1986-87 *Patricia Judith Gallery*, Boca Raton, FL
1969   *Hi-Fi Associates*, Miami, FL
1964   *Contemporary Arts Gallery*, New York University, New York, NY
1963   *Granite Gallery*, East 57th Street, New York, NY
1962   *Key Gallery*, East 57th Street, New York, NY
1961   *Everson Museum*, Syracuse, NY

Special Projects

1983   WGBH-TV, Boston (sets for *Frontline* and *Nova*)
1982-83 WBZ-TV, Boston (sets, including world map)

Public Collections

The Whitney Museum, New York, NY
General Electric, New York, NY
Raytheon Corporation, New York, NY
Continental Can, New York, NY
Air Products and Chemicals, Inc., PA
Datamore, Inc., New York, NY

Data Processing, Inc., Rochester, NY

Grants
1979   "Ecology through Art," video production.

DOROTHY TANNER

Solo Shows
1997   *Museum of New Arts*, Fort Lauderdale
1986-87   *Patricia Judith Gallery*, Boca Raton, FL
1969   *Hi-Fi Associates*, Miami, FL
1964   *Contemporary Arts Gallery*, New York University, New York, NY
1963   *Granite Gallery*, East 57th Street, New York, NY
1962   *Key Gallery*, East 57th Street, New York, NY
1961   *Everson Museum*, Syracuse, NY

Special Projects
1983   WGBH-TV, Boston (sets for *Frontline* and *Nova*)
1982-83   WBZ-TV, Boston (sets, including world map)

Commissions
Club Liquid, Las Vegas, NV
Desks, Inc., Fifth Avenue, New York, NY
Sheraton Hotel, La Guardia Airport, New York
Hilton Hotels, Florida
Loew's Hotels,Grand Bahamas
Fingers, Caracas, Venezuela (private club)
The Library, Lexington, KY (restaurant)
Bemelman's, Miami, FL (restaurant)
Golden Lion, Boston, MA (restaurant)
House of Mo-Ko, Miami, FL (executive offfices)
Scandia, Miami, FL (installation)

Hi-Fi Associates, Miami, FL (installation)
20th Century Fox, Los Angeles, CA
Borkan Residence, North Miami Beach, FL

Public Collections
General Electric, New York, NY
Raytheon Corporation, New York, NY
Continental Can, New York, NY
Air Products and Chemicals, Inc., PA
Datamore, Inc., New York, NY
Data Processing, Inc., Rochester, NY
Damiano, Inc., Syracuse, NY

Grants
1979   "Ecology through Art," video production.

ABOUT THE EDITOR

Michael Betancourt is an experimental film and video artist; art theorist and author. He runs the only avant-garde film and video blog at Cinegraphic.net.

His writings have been published in *Leonardo, Art Scene, C-Theory, Tout-fait* and the *Miami Art Exchange*. His academic writing includes new work on Marcel Duchamp, Francis Bacon, Salvador Dali and many others.

Betancourt's other titles from WildsidePress.com include: *Re-Viewing Miami, Two Woman and a Nightengale, Artemis, and Mary Hallock-Greenwalt: The Complete Patents.*He is the editor of *Visual Music Instrument Patents Vols. I, II,* a compendium of designs for color organs ranging from Bainbridge Bishop's 1876 design through Oskar Fischinger's *Lumigraph.*

www.ingramcontent.com/pod-product-compliance
Lightning Source LLC
Chambersburg PA
CBHW021234090426
42740CB00006B/528